Jerry,

Congrats upon this large & important milestone. May this book be a reminder that we need to live day by day with the Master.

DAY BY DAY
WITH THE MASTER

We appreciate your life and witness. A special love from all of us.

The Pinnos

Don, Marcella
Davy, Brent & Corinnea

DAY BY DAY
WITH THE MASTER

DONALD F. ACKLAND

BROADMAN PRESS
NASHVILLE, TENNESSEE

ISBN: 0-8054-5196-X

Dewey Decimal Classification: 242.2

Subject Headings: DEVOTIONS, DAILY // BIBLE. N.T. GOSPELS

Library of Congress Catalog Number: 83-70209

Printed in the United States of America

Library of Congress Cataloging in Publication Data

Ackland, Donald F.
  Day by day with the Master.

  1. Devotional calendars—Baptists. 2. Bible.
N.T. Gospels—Meditations. 3. Jesus Christ—
Meditations. I. Title.
BV4811.A28   1985   242'.2   83-70209
ISBN 0-8054-5196-X

For
Hazel, Bryan, and Roy—
dear children whose love
for us and for one another
adds sweetness to life

Major Periods
In the Life of the Master

Introduction

By the time a man has passed his eightieth milestone, he has gathered a lot of baggage, some to be discarded, some preserved. If he has spent his life browsing among books, never far from the smell of printer's ink, rubbing shoulders with saints and sinners, and deepening his (and, he trusts, others') knowledge and love for the sacred Scriptures, he should have something worthy to share. This book is sent on its way with its two predecessors, *Day by Day with John* and *Day by Day with the Prophets,* in the hope that what it shares, in contemplation of the life and ministry of our Lord, may have values for others.

Around AD 170, a man named Tatian produced a book with the title *Diatessaron,* a Greek musical term for four-part harmony. This was the first attempt at synthesizing the accounts of the life of Jesus as found in the four Gospels. The same task has been attempted many times since, and new "harmonies" of the Gospels continue to appear. All who have contributed to this useful area of New Testament study have acknowledged difficulties in bringing chronological order to the incidents recorded by Matthew, Mark, Luke, and John. The very nature of these inspired narratives provides the reason. The four evangelists were not committed to writing biographies of Christ but to bearing witness to Him as Savior and Lord.

Having already provided devotional comments on the Fourth Gospel in my book, *Day by Day with John,* this new volume focusses on the Synoptic Gospels as it seeks to furnish daily readings and meditations on the life and ministry of Jesus. For readers who wish to include John's distinctive contribution to the ongoing record, that apostle's major additions to the story are indicated at intervals throughout these pages. The selections from the other three Gospels, arranged as nearly as possible in chronological order, have been made in the interests of continuity, clarity, and significance of detail.

Donald F. Ackland

Nashville, 1984

Gabriel in Galilee ✓
Luke 1:26-38

Here begins the greatest story ever told. We have read it
or listened to it being read so often that its wonder may have
become dimmed. But the wonder is still there. May God
help us to discover it anew and thrill as never before to the
good news that we call the gospel.

In the Bible record of creation, there is a man named
Adam at center stage. In the New Testament's unfolding of
redemption's plan, a woman named Mary is in the spotlight.
There is a man in her story, but he is an obscure figure,
relegated to the shadows. We know his name: Joseph, his
native city: Nazareth, his occupation: carpenter, but little
more. It is as though a voice would say to us: the man whom
God made has failed. If the tragedy of created things is to
be reversed, this must be accomplished by some other than
he. Stand aside, therefore, marvel and see how God will
make a new beginning without the help of man.

The importance of the occasion is revealed in the person
of the messenger. According to Jewish belief, Gabriel par-
ticipated in the burial of Moses. Who was more appropriate,
then, to announce the approaching birth of the Savior? Having interred the Old Testament representative of the law, the
same heavenly being proclaimed the advent of Him who
would bring deliverance from its authority. "For the law was
given by Moses, but grace and truth came by Jesus Christ"
(John 1:17). Another narrator of these events puts the message right on the doorstep of our need when he said of the
Promised One, "He shall save his people from their sins"
(Matt. 1:21).

The Caesar and the Child
Luke 2:1-7

Augustus was an assumed name. The man who bore it was born Octavian, the adopted son of Julius Caesar. He was the first of Rome's parade of emperors. His ascent to power led the incomparable Virgil to hail him as "the man, the one who has been promised again and again." When the senate conferred on him the title of Augustus, one worthy of reverence and worship, the way was opened to claims that here was more than a man. The deification of the Caesars had begun.

Emperors made decrees, and common people carried them out. Luke, himself a Gentile, must have relished the opportunity to tell how the mighty Augustus was used to provide the circumstances in which the true "One who has been promised again and again" would come to birth. As a result of the census which Augustus ordered, a couple with royal family background but now reduced to humble conditions journeyed from Nazareth to Bethlehem. There, again in fulfillment of promise, the child was born whom Gabriel had described as "the Son of the Highest," chosen successor to "the throne of his father David" (1:32).

Fourteen years after the birth of Jesus, Augustus died. His expressed hope that "the foundations which I have laid will last immovable" were doomed to early disappointment. But the name of Bethlehem's child lives on, enshrined in the hearts of multitudes, and the bounds of His kingdom reach far beyond the frontiers of Rome's empire in its strength. The throne of the Caesars is empty. But of God's Christ, the proclamation has gone forth that "his dominion is an everlasting dominion, which shall not pass away" (Dan. 7:14).

Paradox of the Nativity
Luke 2:8-20

"Let no man make his son a muleteer, a camel driver, a barber, a sailor, a shepherd, an innkeeper, forasmuch as their crafts are crafts of robbers." How widely this saying was accepted among first-century Jews, we cannot tell, but there is other evidence that shepherds were among the social outsiders of those times. We should not miss the significance of the presence of both an innkeeper and shepherds in the nativity scenes with which our Lord's story begins. For at the heart of Luke's Gospel is the statement, "I came not to call the righteous, but sinners to repentance" (5:32).

The shepherds are part of the paradox of Bethlehem. Christina Rosetti recognized that paradox when she wrote, "Love came down at Christmas,/ Love all lovely, Love Divine." Reginald Heber expressed it in his contrasting lines, "Low lies His head with the beasts of the stall, . . . Maker, and Monarch, and Saviour of all." E. H. Sears called us to see this paradox by teaching us to sing about "angels bending near the earth,/ To touch their harps of gold." At Bethlehem, heaven and earth touched hands beside a humble manger as angel messengers proclaimed to despised shepherds the glad news of "God and sinners reconciled."

None can be surprised at the reception given to the shepherds' story. "All they that heard it wondered" (2:18). Well they might! For never before nor since has such evidence been given of the condescending love of God as it breaks down all barriers to open up a way of communication between earth and heaven. Angels, shepherds, and "Christ the Lord. . . . lying in a manger" are all part of the paradox that, for believing hearts, is not so much a problem as cause for loudest praise.

Watchers in the Temple
Luke 2:25-38

What a pity that both Simeon and Anna had to be old! Were there none among the younger set in Israel who shared their expectation of the coming Messiah? Probably there were many. But you would have found them elsewhere than in the Temple, more likely in some secret hideaway standing guard over a cache of weapons ready for use against the hated Roman army of occupation. For one tragedy of the world into which Jesus came was that it was looking for a Deliverer, not a Savior.

An obvious explanation of Simeon's concept of the Messiah was his acquaintance with the Old Testament Scriptures. Quotations from the Psalms and the prophets sprang to his lips as he sought words with which to honor the holy babe cradled in his arms. Here was a man who had allowed the Word of God to shape his thinking. Consequently, at a point in his nation's history when most thought of the coming One in narrow, racial terms, this veteran watchman expressed a hope for "all people" to be realized in Him who had come as "a light to lighten the Gentiles, and the glory of thy people Israel" (vv. 31-32).

Equally remarkable was Simeon's understanding of the mission of Jesus. Where could Simeon have gained the insights which enabled him to speak of "a sign which men reject" (v. 34, NEB), with an even more sinister reference to a sword? Surely, from no other source than Isaiah whose pronouncements spelled death for our Savior and life for us. "For the transgression of my people was he smitten" (Isa. 53:8). To know God's Word is to understand the mission of God's Son.

An End and a Beginning ✓
Matthew 2:1-12

Among many legends that have attached themselves to our Lord's nativity, perhaps one only has any claim on our serious interest. The king of Persia, according to this story, had gone into the temple of Ahura Mazda to light the holy flame where he learned of the impending birth of a child who would be known as "The End and the Beginning." The king sent a group of Magi with gifts for this child. After they had presented the gold, frankincense, and myrrh, Mary wanted to give them something in return. All she could offer was one of the swaddling bands the infant Jesus had worn. To the Persian king, the only appropriate use for this sacred cloth was to dedicate it in sacrifice to Ahura Mazda. It was committed to the flames on the temple altar, but after the fire died down, the swaddling band was found whole and unscorched.

This story may lack factual authenticity, but it does not lack truth. The child of Bethlehem has outlasted Ahura Mazda. The message of His birth, the ministry of His life, and the marvel of His death and resurrection are proclaimed and accepted in many places where pagan altars have given place to Christian churches. He came to put an end to the half-truths of artificial religions and to be in Himself the beginning of a revelation by which groping humanity could bask in the full truth of a loving Heavenly Father.

Although Wise Men sought a child whose birth would fulfill Jewish prophecy and Gentile hope, that birth was not a consummation but an introduction. Winston Churchill referred to a situation as "neither the end, nor even the beginning of the end, but rather the end of the beginning." In Christ, the end of prophetic anticipation was designed to be the beginning of unending redemptive blessing.

Refuge in Egypt ✓
Matthew 2:13-23

How strange that the infant Christ should find sanctuary in Egypt and face danger in Judea! Yet this reversal of roles was to become a pattern of the future. As the message of the Son of God incarnate spread throughout the world, ancient enmities were put away while unnatural animosities were kindled to flare with unbridled fury.

The reconciling Christ addresses a deep need in the world of today. He who found refuge in the land of Israel's former bondage also broke through the hostility that existed between Jew and Samaritan, responded to the pleas of despised Canaanites, befriended members of the hated Roman army of occupation, and associated redemptively with outcasts of many kinds. He not only spoke of love but became its embodiment as He built bridges of cordiality across chasms of estrangement. What but His gospel can heal the divisions that continue to threaten the peace of our world? What but His love, interpreted through His people, can be the salve to relieve the pain of suffering multitudes?

Yet, even as we affirm His ministry of reconciliation—and ours—we must deal with His startling statement, "I came not to bring peace, but a sword" (Matt. 10:34). Across His infancy was flung the shadow of that cross on which He would die, rejected by His own people. That such men as Gandhi and Martin Luther King were slain by assassins' bullets is a cruel reminder of the price that must often be paid by those who zealously seek the good of others. Only Jesus, however, could say of His life, "No man taketh it from me, but I lay it down of myself" (John 10:18).

Where Are the Children? ✓

Luke 2:40-52

In parts of our country, television programs are interrupted periodically to flash on the screen a public service statement that reads, "Parents, do you know where your children are tonight?" The purpose is to challenge parents, some of whom may be complacent about their children's moral welfare, to take steps to protect them from harmful activities and companions.

In Christian homes, not complacency but false assumption may be the danger. A loved child is not made the subject of spiritual concern or approach because of the mistake of "supposing him to have been in the company." It is even possible to accept a mistaken doctrine of the family that claims the salvation of the young merely because of parentage. Unfortunately, experience with the unpredictability of human nature forces the conclusion that grace does not run in the blood. Godly people do not necessarily have godly offspring.

The quest for the missing Jesus was delayed for a day because of a wrong conclusion; but once it began, it was thorough. By it, Mary and Joseph showed their worthiness to be the guardians of this world's most precious child. His welfare was more important to them than a pleasant journey home in the company of fellow pilgrims. They found Him where they had left Him, in the Temple. How did He get there? They had taken Him there, and the Spirit within the boy Jesus had responded to all that He saw and heard. He was, as He said, "in my Father's house" (v.49, RSV). Is there any better place for a child to be? Who, then, will take him or her there?

High Endorsement ✓
Matthew 3:1-6,13-17

American visitors to Britain's capital city are often intrigued by a royal coat of arms mounted above the entrance to a store with this accompanying inscription, "By Royal Appointment." The proprietor of this particular store has the honor of having members of the royal family among his customers, and he wants the world to know it. The displayed heraldry is an endorsement of his product from the highest level in the land.

John the Baptizer was surprised when Jesus presented Himself for baptism along with others who were submitting to a rite that publicly declared their repentance for sins committed. Although a fuller understanding of Jesus' person still lay in the future for John, he knew enough about his younger kinsman's moral and spiritual stature to feel a sense of embarrassment. "I need to be baptized by you, and do you come to me?" (v. 13, RSV). But Jesus insisted. He must set His own seal of approval on John's mission and message by taking His place, though sinless, with those who came seeking forgiveness.

This gracious endorsement of the Baptizer's role in God's redemptive plan set the scene for a divine endorsement of Jesus Himself. The days of obscurity in Nazareth were at an end. The incarnate Christ had Himself taken the step that would launch Him on His saving mission. And that all might know that what He was about to do had the full approval of the Father, a dove descended, and a voice resounded. "This is my beloved Son, in whom I am well pleased" (v. 17).

News of Victory Won ✓
Luke 4:1-13

There seems to be no other reasonable conclusion than that the story of the wilderness temptations was told by Jesus Himself. Matthew, Mark, and Luke all make reference to it. The unnamed author of Hebrews must have had it in mind when, having paid glowing tribute to the incarnate Son of God, he added the encouraging words, "For in that he himself hath suffered being tempted, he is able to succour them that are tempted" (Heb. 2:18).

When, might we suppose, did Jesus share with His disciples His experiences when alone in the wilderness He entered into confrontation with the enemy of souls? Was it soon after they were recruited into discipleship? They had taken a giant step of faith in him as Israel's Messiah and were elated at the prospect of future service. They needed to know that Satan takes advantage of our emotional and spiritual highs, and moves in quickly to disillusion, discourage, and defeat. But their Master had triumphed in His time of testing. So might they, and so may we.

Or was it at the point where the disciples were about to become apostles, and privilege was to give way to responsibility that Jesus shared the good news of His victory over satanic pressures? The prospect of losing His companionship bore down heavily upon them. They had failed Him often, even when He was at their sides. What possibility was there of winning with Jesus gone and the world ever present? Perhaps then He told them of His lonely battle against His enemy and theirs. Led by the Spirit and empowered by the memorized Word of God, He had emerged unscathed from the conflict. So might they. So may we.

(If you desire to read John's contribution at this point see pages 14-29 in *Day by Day with John* by Donald F. Ackland, a Broadman Book.)

Christ in Others ✓
Luke 4:14-31

April 2, 1739, is a date to remember. On that afternoon, outside the city of Bristol, England, John Wesley preached for the first time away from a church building. The struggle to break from formality and tradition had been long and stressful. But this Anglican clergyman, exercised in spirit over the unevangelized masses who were unreached by the parish churches, eventually overcame his distaste for "this strange way of preaching" and addressed some 3,000 people "from a little eminence in a ground adjoining the city." His text? "The Spirit of the Lord is upon me, because he hath anointed me to preach the gospel to the poor." (v. 18).

Isaiah was first to use these words, and although they were messianic in nature, they had real significance for the prophet himself. He, too, was a man who, under the Spirit's constraint, had abandoned the security of his upbringing to become God's messenger to a people in deep trouble. Isaiah's call came to him in the sacred precincts of the Temple. But his mission took him before kings and commoners as he exposed sin and warned of judgment to come. Yet his was essentially a message of reconciliation and restoration, addressed to "the brokenhearted" and "the captives."

Centuries before the coming of Jesus, and centuries afterward, two men so closely identified with Jesus' spirit and mission that they could speak of themselves in terms that, in their fullest sense, applied only to Him. When Jesus' compassion possesses us, and His Spirit motivates, we may become reflections, however weak, of our glorious Lord.

A Fish Story ✓

Luke 5:1-11

Our Lord's teaching began with the crowds on the shore and continued with the disciples in the boat. He probably resorted to the use of Peter's boat to put distance between Himself and His thronging listeners. Then, when He had spoken God's word to that larger number, He turned His attention to the small group of fishermen for whom He had great future plans.

Any fisherman worth the name, who returns home empty-handed, hates to talk about his lack of success. How skillfully Jesus obtained Peter's acknowledgement of a night spent on the water without one fish to show for it! Often He must start with our acceptance of failure before He can offer His help. Only when we know our own insufficiency are we likely to avail ourselves of His never-failing power.

Peter and his fishing buddies found themselves beaten at their own game. Nets that had repeatedly come up empty quickly filled to the breaking point when lowered in response to the Master's command. And Jesus, instead of dwelling on earlier failure, recognized their abilities by challenging them with a greater task: "From henceforth thou shalt catch men" (v. 10).

A beloved Methodist preacher and educator, Thomas Champness, asked, "Do you think the Lord Jesus would have called Peter, James, and John to be fishers of men if they had not been good fishermen and knew how to catch fish?" The best preparation for kingdom service may be a job well-done, a family well-served, or a life dedicated to good performance, as Champness said, as a farmer, a blacksmith, or a schoolteacher.

Day to Be Remembered ✓
Mark 1:21-34

Someone in Capernaum that day was doubtless told, "You don't know what you missed by not being at the service this morning." For, in the early hours of the sabbath, Jesus visited the synagogue where He both taught and healed. Then He went home with Peter and Andrew where He healed again and afterward was waited on by the dear woman He had restored to health. The total scene challenges the imagination, for this was a day to be remembered. In church and home Jesus was, first of all, present, as He should always be. Then in both places He revealed His compassion and power so that those who heard and saw were given precious memories that lingered.

This was not only in Peter's home, but the story of what happened that day has come to us from Peter's well-stored mind. How natural that he should retain a vivid picture of what Jesus did within those humble walls and, after sunset, around the lowly door! May all our homes provide such blessed memories! That Peter thrilled to his recollections of his home graced by his Master is evident in his statement that "all the city" came for healing. No charge of exaggeration is allowable, for through his open door that day Peter saw not only a city but a world of people who would be blessed by a word or a touch.

Hymnist Henry Twells caught Peter's spirit in 1868 when he concluded his beautiful hymn with this stanza:

> Thy touch has still its ancient pow'r;
> No word from thee can fruitless fall;
> Hear, in this solemn evening hour,
> And in thy mercy heal us all!

Miracles and Mission ✓
Mark 1:35-45

John Brunton, a distinguished engineer, wrote of his experiences in India: "The natives have an idea that all English sahibs are doctors, and can cure all diseases. Of course I was one in their estimation, and crowds of the natives thronged around my camp, bringing their sick on *charpoys,* or stretchers, expecting me to cure them. The halt, the lame, and the blind were there; how I wished that I could heal them all."

The crowds that surged around Jesus were not stimulated by superstitious hopes but by visual evidence of His powers. Evening healings in Capernaum led to a growing reputation for His compassionate response to human need. The surprising thing is that our Lord made every effort to get away from the clamoring multitudes. After He had healed the leper, He charged Him to "say nothing to any man" (v. 44). Unlike modern faith healers who seek publicity for their claimed successes, this gracious Physician discouraged talk about His merciful deeds. He made the reason clear—His words were more important than His works. Anything that interfered with the free proclamation of the good news He had come to bring, though worthy in itself, must be discouraged.

Is it possible for Christians, as individuals or in churches, to force into second place that to which our Lord gave absolute priority? Any activity, however beneficial to others, that fails to take into account humanity's basic need for spiritual renewal must be regarded as of minor importance to the dissemination of the message that "Christ Jesus came into the world to save sinners" (1 Tim. 1:15).

A Rebound of Blessing ✓
Mark 2:1-12

Five men were blessed that day: the paralytic on his pallet and the four who, by their determination to get their friend to Jesus, shared in the joy of the paralytic's healing. The statement that "they were all amazed, and glorified God" would seem to encompass more even than these five (v. 12). But theirs was a special satisfaction, a deep and personal sense of elation, for together this quintet had sought and obtained the outcome they most desired.

It must always be so. Prayers of intercession invariably set in motion divine forces that enrich the lives of all concerned. To seek the advantage of someone else, specially when that advantage is spiritual in substance, is to make sure of a rebound of blessing. In His exhortation to His disciples to enlarge their prayers to include friendly neighbors and spiteful enemies alike, Jesus added, "That ye may be the children of your Father which is in heaven" (Matt. 5:43-45). That family likeness of which Jesus spoke is as much likely to be the result of such selfless prayer as the motivation for it.

A beloved German evangelical, Sister Eva of Friedenshort, told the story of Tämbring. He was a self-styled atheist. Left by his sister in charge of a dying child, he was embarrased to have the little one say, "Uncle, pray for me to get well." He could not comply. "Uncle, if you don't pray I shall die" came the insistent plea. Tämbring fell on his knees beside the bed and cried, "O God, if there be a God, hear me." The sick child smiled, turned on his side, and went to sleep. The uncle went to his room, locked himself in, and came out a new man to bear a lifelong testimony to Christ's power to save.

Round Pegs in Round Holes ✓
Matthew 9:9-17

Luke also records this event. He says of Matthew (whom he knew as Levi), that he "left all, rose up, and followed him" (Luke 5:28). Some have had the temerity to modify Luke's statement. He left all, they tell us, with one exception. He took with him, from the tax gatherer's office, his pen and ink. In Matthew, the Master recruited a secretary so that it could be said of him, to quote an early Christian source, that he "took down [Christ's] sayings . . . and everyone interpreted them as he was able."

Certainly, Matthew brought to discipleship acquired skills gained from serving the Roman government. We have evidence of his ability as a writer in the Gospel that bears his name. Having accepted a new loyalty, Matthew made his contribution to the cause of Christ by faithfully recording those things he both heard and saw and, with some probable obligation to others, produced a narrative that blesses us to this day.

G. Campbell Morgan, whose abilities as a Bible expositor were recognized on both sides of the Atlantic, said that while Jesus recruited Peter and his Galilean friends by offering to make them "fishers of men" (Matt. 4:19), he did not make that approach to him. "I loved teaching," Morgan said, "so, when Jesus confronted me, he said, 'Follow me, and I will make you a teacher of men.' " Since our Lord has need for all types of workers, He first chooses and then calls persons of varying aptitude that He may match each individual to an appropriate task. For us the question is: Am I willing to devote those talents and skills that I possess to the service of the greatest of all Masters?

Breaking the Rules
Matthew 12:1-8

There is a world of difference between "rules are made to be broken," and "a rule must never be broken." In both cases, the pertinent question is: "Who made the rules?" Any regulation that is established by recognized authority merits the utmost respect. By the same token, any directive or prohibition that is of questionable origin, and destructive of the human spirit, invites criticism and ultimate disregard.

F. F. Bruce, in his book *Tradition: Old and New,* quotes Lewis Carroll's *Alice in Wonderland.* The king gave the command for "all persons more than a mile high to leave the court." He said this was rule forty-two and yet insisted that it was the oldest rule in the book. Alice accused the king of having just invented it. If it was the oldest rule in the book, she asked, why wasn't it number one?

Rule number one on the sabbath was given by God at Sinai. But to it had been added a quantity of restrictions comprising the "oral law" which by our Lord's day had become burdensome and even nonsensical. It was these man-made embellishments against which Jesus protested by reminding His critics that God's guidelines are intended for our good. They are not heavy, and should not be made so by overly zealous persons who play God by adding their own "thou shalt nots."

Most of us are broad-minded in our application of biblical principles to ourselves, ever grateful for loopholes (real or imagined) which give us freedom to do as we please. But how do we treat others? If by accusation or suggestion we try to impose on people standards that exceed God's demands, we misrepresent Him and may create resentments that could lead to disbelief.

Better Than a Sheep?
Matthew 12:9-21

A cynical answer has been given to our Lord's question: "How much then is a man better than a sheep?" (v. 12). That answer sets in sharp contrast the heartless greed of which we humans can be guilty and the self-sacrificing compassion of our Savior. "How much better?" was His question, and this was the callous retort: "It all depends on the price of wool."

What set of values should we use in determining our relationship to and responsibility for others? Certain Pharisees followed a religious set of values. Because the conduct of Jesus violated their rigid code of sabbath observance, they were outraged to the point of plotting His death. It mattered not to them that a once-crippled man had been restored to physical wholeness. They placed a higher value on a set of rules than on the bodily condition of a person changed from helpless dependency to renewed usefulness. In consequence, they were stripped of their robes of self-righteousness and exposed in the nakedness of their hypocrisy.

"How much then is a man better than a sheep?" Men, women, and even children have been sacrificed on the altar of commercial gain. Racehorses, prize cattle, and show dogs are often treated with lavish care while families starve for want of food, and babies die for lack of medical attention. Economic and sociopolitical theories that regard the poor and underprivileged as deserving their plight, and not as victims worthy of discerning help, can only do so by ignoring the Master's question. Nothing is of greater value in the sight of God than a person made in His own image. Did He not send His Son among us to make this very clear?

Night of Decision ✓
Luke 6:12-19

The decisive battle of England's civil war was fought at Marston Moor where the royalist army was routed by the forces of Parliament led by Oliver Cromwell. His biographer, John Buchan, records that on the eve of the battle, Cromwell withdrew from his comrades-in-arms. He was later discovered in a disused room, at the top of a tower, fervently engaged in prayer with his open Bible before him.

Thanks to Luke, we know that our Lord, before choosing His disciples, "went out into a mountain to pray, and continued all night in prayer to God" (v. 12). He was about to select those on whom, with the Spirit's help, would depend the success of that universal plan of redemption to which He and His Father had made full commitment. Any error of judgment in this work of selection might jeopardize the future of His gospel. In characteristic dependence on His Heavenly Father, Jesus withdrew to the solitude of a mountaintop that He might there engage in uninterrupted prayer.

There are three listings of the twelve in the Gospels. All begin with Peter and end with Judas with a tragic concluding comment such as "which also was the traitor" (v. 16). Of all the choices made that night this, surely, was the hardest. For in naming Judas, our Lord gave a man of dangerous potential an opportunity to make good. On the other hand, He exposed Himself to the risk that Judas might be the means of bringing about His death. There were others He could have chosen. But in complete surrender to His Father's will, He chose Judas and thus embraced the cross for you and me.

Jesus' touch

Happiness Is_____?
Matthew 5:1-12

Some like to play "Knock-knock," others the more sophisticated game of "Happiness is _____." To score in the latter you add a word or a phrase. Be careful, however, for in so doing you may reveal something of your character and lifestyle. "Happiness is a small puppy" is child's play, but more adult ambitions reveal themselves in "Happiness is a hole in one," or, "Happiness is a diamond ring," or, "Happiness is a condominium by the sea."

Jesus did not include such things in His concept of happiness. He talked about the felicity of the poor, those that mourn, persons who are hungry and thirsty for righteousness, and, most surprising of all, the persecuted. In nothing He ever said, perhaps, did He more clearly emphasize the difference between the children of this world and the children of God. For He set heaven's highest value on experiences and conditions from which we mortals naturally shrink. If, He said, you would seek the best in this life and the next (for the kingdom of heaven overlaps both), think not first of your own welfare but of God's will, not of how to achieve security and comfort, but how to live faithfully regardless of the cost.

Perhaps Jesus was not talking of happiness in the popular sense. Pity the poor translators who run into Bible words for which there are no adequate English equivalent! "Fortunate" and "how happy" are two of the alternatives offered for "blessed." Maybe nearest to the Master's meaning is "how blest" (NEB), for He was speaking of those who, in spite of apparent adverse circumstances, live under the approval of God. That is life at its best.

Let It Shine! ✓
Matthew 5:13-20

Some parts of our country were subjected to the necessity for blackouts during critical periods of World War II. Those who tried to make their homes lightproof (or was it dark-proof?) experienced the almost impossibility of confining light when it wanted to get out and make its presence known. In one European city, where blackouts were rigidly enforced, two air-raid wardens tracked down an offending shaft of light to a room in a poor apartment house. Inside they found an old lady propped up in bed, reading her Bible by the light of a candle. "I didn't know my light was shining," she pleaded.

That light should ever be suppressed is contrary to the laws of nature and the purposes of God. For the Lord began His work of creation by commanding, "Let there be light," and, as a consequence, "there was light." Moreover, "God saw the light, that it was good" (Gen. 1:3-4). That goodness had its fullest expression in Him whose name is Light and of whom it is written that his "light shines in the darkness, and the darkness has not overcome it" (John 1:5, RSV).

But the darkness has tried and is still trying. In different parts of the world today, attempts are being made to extinguish the light of truth. Yet it persists and prevails, so that even the gloom of official atheism is penetrated by beams of truth as faithful souls, often at appalling risk to themselves, obey their Master's orders: "Let your light . . . shine" (v. 16). Sad, isn't it, that so many of us challenge the darkness with only a flickering wick?

Counsel of Perfection?
Matthew 5:38-48

Using that irresistible logic with which he approached most subjects, C. S. Lewis acknowledged that some of our Lord's discipleship demands appear to be unreasonable: loving one's enemies, for example, which involves the ultimate degree of forgiveness. How do you ask this of a Jew who has known the horrors of Dachau or Buchenwald? Or of a Pole who has been tortured by the Gestapo?

Lewis raised his questions against the background of World War II. But then, placing the issue in a personal context, he confessed that he did not know what he would do in similar circumstances. So—and this is what makes his writings so practical and helpful—he suggested that, instead of exercising ourselves over extreme cases, we begin with our own everyday relationships. If we seek God's help in applying Christ's command "Love your enemies" to the unhappy frictions of family, business, and social life, and if by God's grace we succeed, we shall experience both the difficulty and reward of Christian obedience.

After all, Jesus did not say that these things would be easy. He talked about perfection—a shocking word for most of us—and said, "Aim for that!" We chip away at this word, trying to blunt its sharp cutting edge, thus diluting His challenge to behave as "children of your Father which is in heaven" (v. 45). Yet one of His most loyal followers had the right idea when he confessed to shortcomings in his Christian life, but nevertheless expressed his resolve to reach for "the high calling of God in Christ Jesus" (Phil. 3:14).

Right Made Wrong ✓
Matthew 6:1-8,16-18

Nobody could find fault with generosity, prayer, or self-discipline, least of all the Master. Generosity is both commanded and commended throughout the Bible. Prayer is the expected activity of all who know God. Self-discipline has the endorsement of prophets and apostles who denied themselves physically that their spirits might soar in communion with God.

Yet the worthiest activities can be stripped of merit when they are engaged in from the wrong motives. Jesus knew benefactors of others who gave, not from compassion, but for self-promotion. They took care that others knew how much and how often they gave. There were people who were regular in their devotions, but when the hour of prayer came around they were almost always found at the busiest street corner. There they prayed loud and long to draw attention to their piety. There were those who fasted, and to advance their reputation as deeply religious, turned their self-denials into a public performance.

In three devastating indictments our Lord called such persons hypocrites—playactors—and said that their appetite for popular applause would be satisfied; they would be "paid in full." He borrowed a term that belonged to the business world and made it an exposure of the folly of doing right things for wrong purposes. When religious practice is downgraded to a stage production, when good deeds that are intended for the eyes of God are paraded before the eyes of persons, then the perpetrators get what they seek—that and nothing more. They "have their reward" (v. 16); they are paid in full.

Creature Care ✓
Matthew 6:19-34

When Jesus sought to persuade us of the foolishness of worry, he did not use any finely spun theological or philosophical argument but simply said, "Look around you!" Even the most arid area of the earth has some vegetation, and its frozen extremities have their birds. These are witnesses to God's providential care. They do not possess those human skills by which we use seedtime and harvest to our advantage. But their dependence on forces beyond their control is not to their loss, for a benevolent Creator meets their needs for life and survival. In a generous compliment to our humanity the Master asked, "Are ye not much better than they?" (v. 26).

The swallows of Capistrano are not stronger in their homing instinct than the salmon that abound in American waters. Every spring, millions of these fish leave the ocean to start a difficult journey upstream to the places where they were spawned. The regularity of these salmon runs caused consternation in a Northwest state a few years ago when spring returned without the usual migration of fish up a certain tributary of the Columbia River. Some God-given instinct had warned the salmon of disaster ahead. Later that year, Mount Saint Helens erupted spewing lava, rock, and dust over the area and destroying every living thing within its reach.

Nothing Jesus said may be interpreted as assurance of protection from every threat to our comfort or peace. God, after all, is not our refuge *from* trouble but *in* trouble (Ps. 46:1). But our Master clearly taught that the way of faith is to trust the power, wisdom, and love of the Heavenly Father, and in this trust we find release from useless worry.

Measure for Measure? ✓
Matthew 7:1-12

Two farmers traded with one another. One sold butter, the other sold bread. After a while, the farmer who baked the bread noticed that the packages of butter were getting progressively smaller. So he hauled his neighbor into court on the complaint that he was being cheated. The judge ordered the butter-making farmer to bring his scales into court. "Now show me your weights," said the judge. "I have no weights," answered the butter-making farmer. "Then how do you weigh your butter?" he was asked. "I weigh my butter against his bread," was the farmer's reply.

There is a story told about Shammai and Hillel, two Jewish rabbis who lived shortly before the coming of Christ. A Gentile derisively asked them to summarize the Mosaic law while he stood on one foot. Shammai dismissed the man in anger, but Hillel replied, "Do not unto others what you would not have others do to you."

To provide us with an adequate guide for interpersonal relationships, our Lord and Master changed the rabbi's negative statement into a golden positive. "All things whatsoever ye would that men should do to you, do ye even so to them" (v. 12). We could, of course, adopt this policy as a means to self-advantage, expecting others to make life easier for us because we act in kindness to them. But the example of the Master challenges us to a nobler spirit. In His own elaboration of the Golden Rule Jesus said, "Do good, ... hoping for nothing again; ... and ye shall be the children of the Highest" (Luke 6:35). God's indiscriminate kindness should be our pattern, "for he maketh his sun to rise on the evil and on the good" (Matt. 5:45).

False Faces ✓
Matthew 7:13-23

Deception is often hard to detect. A word in common use can be a reminder of this. The word is *sincere,* and it means "without wax." As long ago as Roman times, faults in valuable statuary were concealed by filling holes and other blemishes with wax. Amateur purchasers, who could not distinguish between perfect and imperfect pieces, relied on the word of merchants who declared their statuary to be "without wax." We may be sure that many were defrauded by a practice that took experienced eyes to uncover.

Our Lord warned disciples against false prophets whom He compared to wolves in sheep's clothing, a figure that suggests deliberate disguise. Throughout the centuries, schemers have sought to subvert the unwary by pretending to be what they are not. Some today who claim to be Christian are actually engaged in activities that contradict Christ's teaching. He is not deceived by their false faces, but we may be.

Among Jesse James stories is that of the robbery of a train on which a Baptist deacon was traveling. With Jesse's gun pointed at him, the deacon produced from his pocket a paltry sum. Believing that because of his prosperous appearance the deacon was carrying more money than that, Jesse placed his gun against the man's head and demanded that he empty his pockets. The deacon acknowledged that he was carrying a larger sum but stated that it was the proceeds of a missionary offering which he was carrying to Kansas City. Jesse, as the story goes, put down his gun, stretched out his hand, and said, "Shake, brother, I'm a Baptist, too." But Jesus said, "By their fruits ye shall know them" (v. 20).

Houses and People ✓
Matthew 7:24-29

To a potential buyer, the two houses in our Lord's parable probably looked equally desirable. They may have been built to the same design, and to all intents and purposes they were identical. Only time would reveal that one of the houses had a basic fault. It had a foundation of sand whereas the other rested on solid rock. In the fury of a storm, one house collapsed while its companion stood firm. The Romans had a saying, *Caveat emptor,* which means, "Let the buyer beware." Some there are who learn the wisdom of these words the hard way.

But Jesus, while He talked about houses, was really concerned about people and the kind of foundation their lives are built on. A Christian worker, who had given years to the service of churches, unexpectedly found himself involved in a business relationship. He was thrust into a wider social circle than he was accustomed to and, as he said, began to "rethink his theology" in the light of what he found. Many of his new acquaintances made no profession of faith and yet appeared to be fine human beings. What true difference was there between these and the church people among whom he had been raised and for so long had served?

According to our Lord, a time of testing will come into every life (whether now, or hereafter, who knows?) when external appearances will lose importance, and a person's relationship to Him and His teaching will determine his or her destiny. For the greatest sin before God is unbelief, and the only merit the best of us can claim is that, in the desperation of our lostness, we have listened to His voice and resolved to trust and obey Him.

Equality of Need
Luke 7:1-17

On successive days, a Roman centurion and a bereaved mother had their sorrow turned to joy by the compassionate Christ. While He was on earth, the only condition for the bestowment of His blessing was realized need. He asked no questions about race or social status as He taught us the love of God by the concern He showed for humanity's ills and the power He exerted to give relief.

In nineteenth-century London, people flocked to the office of Dr. John Abernethy, a doctor whose methods were ahead of his time and whose reputation was widespread. Some people thought him rude, yet poor folk seeking his help found him considerate and kind. The wealthy alone complained about his discourtesy. They had to take their turn with other patients. The titled person and his servant entered by the same door, waited in the same room, and received the same attention. That was Dr. Abernethy's way.

In gentler fashion, our Lord taught us that the need of one is the need of all, and the remedy for that need is indiscriminately offered. In Jesus' ministry, physical healing was used to make us aware of His power to cure the more serious maladies of the soul. That He even raised the dead is for us an assurance of the fullness of life that awaits believers on the other side of the grave. Just as the soldier from Caesar's legions had no advantage over the widow of Nain, so rich and poor, high and low, well-known and unknown are made sure of the same gracious reception when they come as suppliants before God in the name of the Lord Jesus Christ.

Release from Doubt ✓
Luke 7:18-30

John the Baptizer was in prison. Incarceration for any person is a harsh experience, damaging to both mind and body. For a man of the wide open spaces, as was John, confinement to the remote fortress of Machaerus must have been unendurable. In the grip of depression, he began to question his own earlier confidence that Jesus was indeed "he that should come" (v. 19) the hope of Israel, and "the Lamb of God" (John 1:29).

John Bunyan, who himself spent twelve years in prison, told in *The Pilgrim's Progress* how Christian and Hopeful were thrown into the dungeon of Doubting Castle, "nasty and stinking to the spirit," and owned by Giant Despair. The two were there "from Wednesday morning till Saturday night . . . far from friends and acquaintances." In his isolation the Baptist shared a similar experience, for his prison was on the far side of the Dead Sea, many miles from the action that accompanied Jesus wherever He was. Christian and his companion found release through prayer. John addressed his doubts directly to Jesus and received an answer that must have dispersed his gloom.

The sunbathed heights of unwavering faith constantly beckon us, and, as sincere followers of our Lord, we strive to scale them. But, try as we may, there are valleys of doubt into which we stumble and from which we can only escape as we call on God to help. Since it was Sunday morning when Christian and Hopeful emerged from Doubting Castle, Bunyan was probably trying to tell us that each recurring Lord's Day affords the prospect of deliverance from whatever ails our spirits. In the worship of our God and the fellowship of His people, we may find the power to start afresh, with quickened step, toward the Celestial City.

When Opportunity Knocks ✓
Matthew 11:20-30

The stubbornness of the human spirit is as amazing as the opportunities that this stubbornness can cause to be lost. No more gracious words exist in Scripture than our Lord's invitation, "Come unto me, all ye that labour and are heavy laden, and I will give you rest" (v. 28). Yet they were uttered in a context of rejection, with consequent warning of impending disaster. Against a background of spurned calls to repentance and pronouncements of coming judgment, the patient Savior renewed His pleas to burdened persons of all time to find rest in Him.

Facing the Excelsior House in the small town of Jefferson, Texas, is the once-resplendent private railroad car of tycoon Jay Gould. That car is a monument to a community's failure to recognize and take advantage of a golden opportunity. Mr. Gould wanted to route his railroad through Jefferson, but the citizens said no. In the guest register of Excelsior House the disappointed promoter wrote, "Grass will grow in your streets. Your buildings will crumble. Your population will disappear." Jefferson was left to its prophesied decline. Jay Gould moved on to another small Texas town named Dallas.

There are opportunities of major proportion that come to us occasionally and either leave us richer or pass us by. Christ's call to faith and obedience is chief among these. But few days go by in any of our lives without opportunities knocking at our door and demanding a decision. How we respond will clearly indicate our goals for the future, whether we are content with short-term gains or are developing a life design for eternity.

In Simon's House ✓
Luke 7:36-50

No sharper contrast can be imagined than the conduct of Simon the Pharisee and that of the unnamed woman "which was a sinner." Why Simon invited Jesus as his guest presents a problem, for he extended to him none of the normal courtesies of a Palestinian host. There must have been an ulterior motive behind his invitation, or a shallow curiosity that was quickly dissipated when our Lord submitted to the woman's anointing.

It is hard to know why some people attend church and even seek church membership. Their presence in God's house may seem as inappropriate as this woman's intrusion on a Pharisee's meal. But our attitude toward them should be determined by our Lord's example. By His acceptance of Simon's invitation He made possible His association with this judgmental man, and did it as graciously as He accepted the attention of the uninvited guest. For Jesus sought the eternal good of both these people and, surprisingly enough, had success with the more unlikely of the two.

Simon's critical nature stood in the way of blessing for him. He classified the woman as a sinner without any insight into her recent experience. He dismissed Jesus as no prophet on grounds that exposed his own deep prejudices. Should it not be cause for alarm that the way we react to others may make or mar our own relationship with God? Simon and his other guests make their exits from this story with a question on their lips that challenged Jesus' authority to forgive sins. The despised intruder, however, left Simon's house with the assurance of forgiveness ringing in her ears.

Improving the Hours

Mark 3:20-30

A bunch of sayings have survived the centuries, all of which can be summed up in one, "A bad beginning makes a bad ending." We must believe this, for we often explain our failures by stating that we "started off on the wrong foot." We account for frustrating days with the confession that we "got out of bed on the wrong side." Are life's beginnings and endings so strongly tied together that one cannot be made to improve on the other?

One day in our Lord's life opened depressingly. There were doubtless many others. But on this particular morning He was met by unbelief on the part of His family ("He is beside himself") and open hostility from His enemies ("He hath Beelzebub") (vv. 21-22). How was that for a discouraging start? But those who have researched the matter tell us that, from an early experience of rejection, our Lord moved forward into hours of marvelous teaching through parables and concluded His day by crossing the lake called Galilee to heal a Gadarene demoniac. A day that began unpromisingly was turned into a triumph of concern for others as people were taught heavenly truths, and one unfortunate creature was set free from satanic bondage.

If there is one word that should describe all Christians, it is the word *overcomers.* By the power of the indwelling Spirit, we can throw off any burden of gloom that circumstances may impose and live victoriously through hours that might otherwise be spent in self-pity and consequent unproductiveness. The promise of our Master is not to shield us from unpleasant experiences but to help us rise above them. As He surmounted misrepresentation and rejection and left the world eternally enriched by His passage through it, so we, with strength beyond ourselves, may turn bad beginnings into glorious endings.

Beware Empty Houses!
Matthew 12:38-45

Empty houses need boarding up; otherwise, they won't stay empty for long. There is something about empty houses that attracts people, usually the worst kind. And if you keep people out, there are other things that can take up residence, so what once was habitable, perhaps beautiful, becomes desolation.

Jesus talked about an empty house to people who asked of him a sign. For them, miracles were not enough. They wanted sensation, not mended limbs, unstopped ears, and blind eyes made to see. Maybe they wished Jesus to divide the Jordan as did His namesake, Joshua. Maybe they sought a sign in the heavens, the sun made to stand still or the moon turned to blood. In all probability they did not know what they wanted, except to embarrass the Savior in front of others. Their demand was empty, as were many of their lives, for they had put reformation in place of regeneration. Through following legal "thou shalt nots," they had rid themselves of their sense of sin but lacked positive deeds of righteousness. They were like empty houses that invite all kinds of undesirable guests who bring ultimate ruin.

Jesus offered Himself as the only sufficient remedy for that emptiness that leads to disaster. Say no to Him, and the chambers of the soul are left open to all kinds of evil. Say yes to Him, and a house becomes a home, the dwelling place of the Son of God. "Behold," He says, "I stand at the door, and knock: if any man hear my voice, and open the door, I will come in to him, and will sup with him, and he with me" (Rev. 3:20).

Family Friction ✓

Mark 3:31-35

How does a person maintain both work and witness for Christ in an environment of family hostility or indifference? John Wesley made one attempt at marriage, but the lack of understanding and support from his wife, Mary, brought that union to an early end. An eminent preacher of the early twentieth century remained married to a woman who not only showed no interest in his work but even succeeded in alienating their daughters. Imagine the preacher who, at the end of a busy Sunday, returns home with no friendly voice to say, "You did well today, John."

No sorrow borne by our Lord could have been greater than that caused by the unbelief of His family. "For neither did his brethren believe in him" (John 7:5). We have recently read how they, and perhaps some of His friends, considered Him "beside himself" (Mark 3:21). Although Jesus' resurrection brought His kinfolk into the community of faith, the years of public ministry were lived in the knowledge that those nearest and dearest to Him (with the exception of His mother) responded in unbelief to His claims.

In our contemporary Christian culture, strong emphasis is placed on family participation in the life of the church. We may have gotten away from the family pew, but parents and children still are encouraged to express a mutual faith by membership of the church and sharing in its worship. This, however, is not universally so. In many parts of the world, profession of faith in Christ means the beginning of a lonely pilgrimage, sometimes made harder by family hostility. As we count our blessings as Christian families, we should be prayerfully aware of the price some pay for discipleship.

The Switch to Parables

Matthew 13:1-9

A nineteen-year-old youth, summoned with little warning to fill a country pulpit, fell back on an illustration he had heard a few weeks before from the lips of a gifted preacher. He had not gone far when a voice was heard from the rear of the building, "Young man, when are you going to quit telling stories and get to preaching?"

The teaching method of the Master raised a similar question on the part of His disciples, "Why speakest thou unto them in parables?" (v. 10). Let it be said to the credit of these men that they were attentive enough to what Jesus said to notice a change in His approach to the listening multitudes. But they were puzzled to know why He, superb teacher that He always was, suddenly departed from a more direct form of preaching and teaching to the use of narrative and illustration. Once committed to this new form of communication, Jesus stayed with it. "All these things spake Jesus unto the multitude in parables; and without a parable spake he not unto them" (v. 34).

Are we not sometimes guilty of elevating inflexibility to a virtue? The attitude of "this-is-how-things-have-been-done-as-long-as-I-remember" has stood in the way of progress in every sphere of life and nowhere more than in the churches. How refreshing it is to find that He whom we take as our infallible instructor did not hesitate to try a new approach when it promised to serve His purpose. Perhaps we need periodically to ask whether the way we do things in worship, evangelism, teaching, and other church activities may not need revision. To reject the new as unacceptable may be to throw opportunity to the winds.

"Lend Me Your Ears"
Matthew 13:10-23

Why did God give us ears? Not for decoration as many of us are aware when we look in a mirror. Ears are for hearing. They are built-in receivers whereby contact is maintained with everything around us that produces sound. They are God's thoughtful equipment whereby we enjoy the music of an orchestra, the song of birds, the message of the gospel, the gurgling chatter of the newborn, and the whisperings of love.

But ears react to other sounds than the beautiful and pleasing. They register the threatening noise of an approaching storm. They stimulate quick reaction to the crack of a gun. In some parts of the world, the strident notes of an air-raid siren send people scurrying to their shelters. Ears are supplied to receive warnings of impending danger as well as to communicate tones that soothe and delight.

"He that hath ears, let him hear" (v. 9), said Jesus, for this shortened form of the saying seems to be the original. Perhaps He was applying a common proverb to the serious business of response to what He had to say. He was concerned for persons who "hearing . . . hear not, neither do they understand" (v. 13). These were condemned, not in advance of their unresponsiveness, but because of it. And to induce them to listen more closely and think more deeply, He laced His teaching with parables. As God's spokesman Jesus felt His own responsibility, but He was careful to emphasize the responsibility of those who listened to what He said. "Nature has given us two ears but only one mouth," wrote Disraeli. If we talked a little less, and listened a little more, we might all be gainers.

Likenesses of the Kingdom ✓
Matthew 13:24-35

God in His wisdom has told us a little, but not much, about heaven. What He has revealed is in terms of the superlative: a city with precious jewels for its foundations, gates made of pearl, streets paved with gold, and walls of jasper. As we marvel at these descriptions, we know that we are being taught about our future home by dazzling imagery. The magnificence of the Father's house is so beyond our mortal comprehension that this world's most valuable (and, for the majority of us, unattainable) treasures can but stimulate our imaginations and enliven our hopes.

But when Jesus talked about the kingdom of heaven, He found His illustrations in the world of common things. He said that it is like a farmer in his field, a man planting a tree, or a woman making bread. Other comparisons He used were equally commonplace, a strong reminder that heaven and the kingdom of heaven are not one and the same. For the kingdom defines the reign of God, something we can enter and experience here and now, and whose conditions may be readily understood through truth revealed in everyday happenings.

Only those who, in this life, submit to the rule of God can have hope of future admission into the home of God. Fortunately, the way into the Kingdom is so plainly defined that a little child can find it. Jesus said, in fact, that to become as a little child is necessary to enter the Kingdom. Even when He used picture language to help our understanding of the Kingdom, Jesus built His pictures from familiar materials that none need be deprived of safe and sure arrival in that "land of pure delight" whose symbols are as uncommon as gold and precious stones.

Surprise or Search?

Matthew 13:36-52

Seventeenth-century diarist Samual Pepys described how, when Holland's navy entered the Thames and its guns were heard all over London, he hurriedly buried his valuables in the ground. He later recovered his treasure, unlike other owners who might have died without the secret of their hidden wealth being revealed. This happened sometimes in Jesus' time. He commended the wisdom of the person who, accidentally discovering buried treasure, sold everything to become its legal owner. But He lifted his story of earthly gain to spiritual heights. His intended reference was to the happiness of those who suddenly realize the importance of the riches of the soul and make every effort to possess them. Unfortunately, persons who will bend over backward to make a good business deal are often unresponsive to the opportunity to become an heir of God's eternal kingdom.

Some search hard and long for the goodly pearl of the gospel as Christ's merchant sought for the jewel of his dreams. In our day, the spiritual pilgrimage of Malcolm Muggeridge matches our Lord's short story. Disillusioned by socialism, outraged by Communism, Muggeridge sought desperately for answers to his questions about ultimate truth. He has told how, while shaving, he was overwhelmed by the desire to be a Christian. He had no deeper wish. Eventually, he found his "pearl of great price" (v. 46) and proved for himself, and for us, the faithfulness of the Bible's promise that "those who seek me diligently find me" (Prov. 8:17, RSV). That word is given special emphasis to us in our Master's assurance, "Seek, and ye shall find" (Matt. 7:7).

Other Little Ships

Mark 4:35-41

One respected commentator writes of the phrase "other little ships" as an "unnecessary reference." But it was not so to the author of this Gospel or to Peter who, besides being with Jesus on the lake, was the probable source of Mark's information. Those "other little ships" figured prominently in his memories of that tempestuous night. Was it because the occupants of those boats joined in the chorus of amazement, "What manner of man is this, that even the wind and the sea obey him?" (v. 41).

On behalf of our quoted commentator, it should be acknowledged that those accompanying boats played no obvious part in the incident and are not even mentioned in parallel accounts in Matthew and Luke. They belonged to the company of the anonymous, yet in some way they served a divine purpose. Think of the "other little ships" of Christian history that have been barely acknowledged, yet have contributed to some grand design! Among them must be included those "other women" who accompanied the Master from Galilee to Jerusalem (Mark 15:41).

John Owen, Bunyan's contemporary, is still considered by many to be the greatest of Puritan divines. As an unconverted man, he attended church one Sunday expecting to hear one of the pulpit orators of the day. But the great man was out of town, and an unknown preacher took his place. The earnestness of the man impressed Owen and, as he developed his text, his listener came under conviction. That text was none other than our Lord's reproving question, "Why are ye so fearful? how is it that ye have no faith?" (v. 40). Later attempts to identify the substitute preacher were unsuccessful. He was one of those "other little ships" who must be content with obscurity, but cannot be dismissed as unnecessary.

Demons and Pigs ✓
Mark 5:1-20

The valuable teaching in Jonah's story can be missed by paying too much attention to the big fish. The Gadarene demoniac's miraculous recovery can be discounted by critical questions over the loss of a herd of swine. T. H. Huxley, writing sarcastically of "the Gaderene pig affair," accused our Lord of unethical conduct for destroying a farmer's livestock. It would seem that some people find it easier to side with those who "began to pray him to depart out of their coasts" (v. 17) than to credit Jesus with a worthy motive in His handling of a desperate case of satanic possession.

Two hundred years ago, a physician to one of the czars of Russia cured that senile monarch of an obsession that he had a bee buzzing in his brain. The doctor extracted a live bee from the monarch's ear, and when the czar saw the bee he immediately felt better. Nobody told him, of course, that the doctor had been guilty of sleight of hand.

Jesus had no need to resort to tricks. The healing of the demoniac was real. The evil powers that had possessed the man were exorcised by the authoritative voice of the Son of God. And that the wretched victim might have visible proof of his deliverance, the swine were sacrificed to a watery death. For He, who once asked, "How much then is a man better than a sheep?" (Matt. 12:12), once again affirmed the value of human personality by giving the lives of animals for a person's return to sanity. In these days, when human life has become cheap and our hearts are in danger of becoming calloused by frequent televised scenes of violent death, the ministry of our Lord to broken minds and bodies should convince us of the Father's high estimate of His children's worth.

"Who Touched Me?" ✓

Mark 5:21-34

Strange—is it not?—that many should see this woman's action as an expression of superstition. She had heard of Jesus, the Healer, and had such abounding faith in Him that she believed the answer to her twelve-year search for health could come through touching His garment. She shunned any vocal appeal for His help, for she was sensitive to the ritual uncleanness of her condition. Not superstition but firm belief that the cure could come from the slightest contact with our Lord, persuaded her to reach out her hand and brush His clothes. The final judgment on her action must be that of Jesus Himself when He said, not "Thy touch hath made thee whole" but, "Thy faith" (v. 34).

We could share the disciples' surprised reaction to their Master's question, "Who touched my clothes?" (v. 30). Jostled by eager crowds He astonished them, and could astonish us, by professing to feel one contact above all others. But we do ourselves better service by recognizing, in this concerned inquiry, impressive evidence of divine response to individual need.

Sometimes, in the prayer-meeting hour when names are mentioned of friends who are sick, and others facing varieties of personal crisis, our minds are baffled to remember all these calls for a place in our intercessions. At other times when praying, we may wonder at our presumption that God will hear us when thousands, even millions, may be petitioning Him at the same time. Could any greater encouragement to the prayer of faith be found than the Master's question, "Who touched me?" Whether we speak to God for ourselves or for others, He is tuned in to our wavelength, and without ignoring others, gives attention to our pleas.

Language of Love ✓
Mark 5:35-43

For many years, Dr. Martyn Lloyd-Jones inspired audiences on both sides of the Atlantic with his Bible expositions and sermons. But people who knew him well would say, "You have never heard him at his best until you have heard him preach in his native Welsh." Since those who speak Welsh regard it as the language of heaven, Dr. Lloyd-Jones's eloquence could have had an out-of-this-world explanation.

When the Jews returned from Babylonian Exile they had adopted a new language, Aramaic, that was to oust Hebrew for everyday use. This was the language Jesus spoke. Although the Gospels were written in Greek, the first-century international tongue, some of our Lord's Aramaic words and phrases were retained. No doubt they conjured up precious memories. That Jesus at prayer addressed his Father as *Abba*, a child's word for his beloved parent, impressed itself on the disciples' minds (Mark 14:36) and was turned to spiritual advantage by the apostle Paul (Rom. 8:15; Gal. 4:6).

One specially cherished memory related to the raising of Jairus's daughter. In the presence of Peter, James, and John, the Master took this child by the hand as He said, "Talitha cumi," Little girl, wake up (v. 41). By these same words the child's parents had aroused her, morning by morning. This was the language of love, so suited to Him who took time to pause in a busy schedule that He might pronounce the gospel charter for all childhood, "Suffer the little children to come unto me, and forbid them not: for of such is the kingdom of God" (Mark 10:14). If only all boys and girls were as responsive to Christ's words as this young daughter of Galilee of whom it is written that "straightway the damsel arose, and walked" (v. 42).

Handicap of Familiarity

Mark 6:1-6

In an interview, Itzhak Perleman, the celebrated violinist, told how as a young musician he became bored with Mendelssohn's *Violin Concerto in E Minor*. This masterpiece was his practice material, and he played it so laboriously and often that he wearied of it. Not until later years did he discover the beauty of this musical gem that now has a prominent place in his repertoire.

When Jesus returned to Nazareth, the scene of His boyhood and young manhood, He suffered rejection at the hands of people who had known Him in His earlier years. To them, He was nothing better than "the carpenter, the son of Mary" (v. 3), whose brothers and sisters were part of the community. Their presumption of knowledge, based on earlier contact with Jesus and Mary's family, worked to their irreparable loss for "he could there do no mighty work" (v. 5).

Sad indeed is the thought that the hands of the healing Christ can be tied by human unbelief. The power to bring relief to the sick and suffering was present, witness the fact that "he laid his hands upon a few . . . and healed them." But that power was put under restraint, and other poor wretches faced futures in bondage to disease and the devil, because of the attitude of those who felt they knew Jesus too well to be deceived by a few miracles.

We are not likely to treat the Master in this way. But there may be a hometown person in the circle of our influence whose purpose in life may be furthered or hindered by the spirit we show toward Him. Bethlehem's shepherd boy, who became Israel's greatest king, attributed his success to God as he exclaimed, "Thy gentleness hath made me great" (2 Sam. 22:36).

A Medley of Men ✓
Matthew 10:1-15

From a larger number of followers, the Master chose twelve to be His close companions, to receive His special instruction, and to become His apostles or commissioned messengers. There are four listings of these in the New Testament of which this is the first. Seven of the names belonged to persons who played recognizable roles in the developing story of Christ and His church. Four are mentioned never to appear again in the inspired record. And one, as Matthew states it, was "Judas Iscariot, who also betrayed him" (v. 4).

It could be a helpful exercise to read each name and ask, "What do I remember about this man?" We would have no difficulty recalling incidents that involved Peter. Andrew, James, John, and Philip would also fare well in our recollections. Thomas, too, and Matthew (who wrote this Gospel) would gain our recognition. As for the others, excluding Judas, we would have difficulty identifying them let alone remembering any part they played in the Bible story.

Yet Jesus chose every one of them, spent time in training them, and included them all in His program of evangelism. That some revealed leadership potential was to be expected. As for the others, it is not possible to feel that they were nonentities upon whom the Master's companionship and teaching was wasted. The little fellow who claimed a measure of dignity, in spite of obvious poverty, said, "God don't make no trash." Our names do not have to be in the headlines for us to make our contribution to the ongoing cause of our Lord and Savior.

Paying the Price ✓
Matthew 10:16-31

As Bible readers, we almost inevitably feel a certain detachment from what we read. Our own country's beginnings seem remote enough, yet Old Testament records go back to those mysterious centuries that we label BC. Even the contents of the Gospels refer to events that happened almost two thousand years ago. So when we read how Jesus warned His disciples of the high cost of loyalty, we may tend to put the whole scenario in the past tense, and leave it there. We may forget that faithful witnesses to Christ have endured grievous hardships down the Christian centuries, and continue to do so now.

One hundred years before Idi Amin terrorized Uganda with his violent misrule, that troubled country was under the heel of a king named Mwanga. A Scottish missionary, Alexander Mackay, had worked with this man's father to improve the lot of his people. Arab slave traders, however, seized on the opportunity of Mwanga's succession to the throne to vent their spite on Mackay and his Christian following. Mwanga ordered these to be burned, and Mackay himself lived in daily expectation of death. Ignoring the pleas of such men as H. M. Stanley, he remained at his work and died in his early forties, a worn-out old man.

But that again, we may say, was one hundred years ago. Contemporary persecution is perhaps more subtle, but no less real. A Russian, for example, on confessing Christ may have this fact recorded in his employment file, thus prejudging his future. Harrassment by the secret police may be a continuing experience. How comfortable are our lives compared to these who pay the price of serving Christ!

Sword or Cup?
Matthew 10:32-42

Which better suits the hand of Jesus, the sword or the cup? Or the hands of those who claim to be His followers? His references to swords were few; yet, from the conduct of some who profess His name, one might suppose that He gave his blessing to these weapons.

Church historian Paul Johnson has revealed how the Crusades of the Middle Ages, when stripped of their pious pretenses, had greed for land and priceless treasures as their true explanation. As proclaimed champions of Christianity, the crusaders perpetrated vicious massacres of Jews and Moslems. Religious relics were considered among the most desirable prizes, so we have the shameful incident on record of Eastern Orthodox priests being tortured to make them part with fragments of the "true cross."

One man, Raymond Lull, had a better idea of what constitutes a crusade. He saw his life mission in terms of reaching Moslems to win them to faith in Christ. His missionary efforts, however, met with bitter opposition. Eventually, he was stoned to death in North Africa in 1315 but not before he had written these beautiful words: "Love bids you ever love—in buying and selling, in weeping and laughing, in speech and in silence, in gain and in loss, in whatsoever you do."

Raymond Lull had caught the spirit of the Master. He places in our hands not a sword, but a cup of cold water, that we may help rather than hurt, heal rather than wound, and bring relief and not pain. In our ministry to others, He would have us show the love that made Him drink Gethesemane's cup, bitter to Him but sweet to all who believe.

Take Time Out!
Mark 6:30-44

Nothing, surely, could make the Gospel story more contemporary than the statement made about Jesus and His disciples, "There were many coming and going, and they had no leisure so much as to eat" (v. 31). What Milton called "the busy hum of men" has been around for a long time though its sound may have become louder as the pace of life has quickened. Yet in Jesus' day, the demands made upon Him and the pressures that surrounded Him made necessary this retreat across the lake to a quiet refuge on the other side.

The Master fully recognized and acknowledged the urgency of His task. "I must work the works of him that sent me, while it is day: the night cometh, when no man can work" (John 9:4). The three short years assigned Him for His public ministry must have seemed all too brief. Yet again and again, He led His disciples away from the clamoring crowds that together they might rest and recuperate for new responsibilities.

Many reasons are offered today for excessive demands on time and strength which, if surrendered to, can turn a person into a workaholic. With this man or woman it is the profit motive that is the driving force. With another it is the commitment to excel in a chosen field. There are people who feel that their dedication to Christ requires that they sacrifice all leisure activities to one grand endeavor. But none can claim the example of the Lord Jesus as justification for this one-sided life-style. The example He gave calls us to recognize the importance of relaxation through which our physical and social needs and obligations may be met.

Frustrated Intentions
Matthew 14:22-33

If the disciples had been left to their own devices, would they have attempted to organize our Lord's time much after the pattern of modern "efficiency" experts? Their impatience with those who brought little children for His blessing indicates that, to their way of thinking, this was not the occasion to bother the Master. Those little ones must wait for the children's hour and not intrude into our Lord's regular schedule. After all, the more important the task in hand, the more important to abide by the rules.

Surprisingly, Jesus seems to have allowed considerable latitude in the use of His time. When on the way to the bedside of Jairus's daughter, He permitted the intrusion of an afflicted woman, granted her heart's desire, and then continued on His way to the deceased child's home. Sometimes His plans for needed rest were interrupted in order for Him to render emergency service. His retreat across the lake was ended when hungry multitudes made claims on His compassion. And although after feeding the five thousand, He returned to His prayer mountain, the plight of His disciples on Galilee's stormy waters brought Him quickly to their rescue.

This is the other side of the Master's regard for physical and mental relaxation. He never stood on His rights in this or any other matter. Service to and for others was His all-possessing purpose. Although He knew the value of occasional release from life's stresses, and captured what periods of quiet and rest He could, our exemplary Savior put others first. When His intentions were frustrated, He transformed frustration into opportunity.

(See *Day by Day with John*, pages 37-42.)

Hygiene or Hypocrisy?
Mark 7:1-13

According to some Europeans, Americans spend too much time doing two things to themselves—weighing and washing. It is hard to argue against this accusation since so many of our bathrooms contain bathroom scales as standard equipment. But our frequent use of showers and scales shows concern for physical health and hygiene, and though these may become regular rituals, they are without religious significance. Not so the washings insisted on by the critics of the disciples. Cleansing of hands and arms had become a matter of spiritual merit. A practice that was only required of priests had been made obligatory for all, so those who neglected it were thought worthy of blame.

What is wrong with washing the hands? Nothing, unless a simple act is so emphasized that it becomes a test of orthodoxy. What is wrong? Nothing, provided what Jesus called "tradition" is not paid more attention than the express commands of Almighty God. Those who sat in judgment on His disciples for neglect of a mere custom were themselves guilty of serious breaches of divine law and family duty. As an example, Jesus exposed a bit of pious chicanery whereby sons and daughters failed in their responsibilities to their parents while gaining credit for generosity to the church. That, he said, makes "the word of God of none effect" (v. 13). To count calories may be commendable, and sometimes necessary, but not at the cost of failing to calculate our obligations to others. To bathe well and often may make us more pleasant to have around, but it is no substitute for a cleansed heart.

Marginal Comment
Mark 7:14-23

Some people have a way of scribbling their thoughts in the margins of books and documents as they read. Winston Churchill, so the story goes, was so exasperated with a typical piece of bureaucratic gobbledygook, which both confused the mind and murdered the king's English, that he added this terse comment: "Up with this I will not put."

We have reputable authority for believing that, early in the transmission of Mark's Gospel, someone made an important annotation at the end of verse 19. This is obscured by the King James Version but comes out clearly in later translations, "Thus he declared all foods clean" (NEB). Who was responsible for this we cannot tell. It could have been Mark himself. Or was it Peter, whose memories of our Lord are preserved in this Gospel?

There is an element of enthusiasm in the words, "Thus he declared all foods clean," that suggests the writer was happy of heart to record his comment. Who had more reason than Peter to rejoice over words of Jesus that finally ended the bondage of Old Testament legalism? At Joppa, his hard-headed allegiance to Mosaic regulations was rebuked by a voice from heaven that said, "What God hath cleansed, that call not thou common" (Acts 10:15). But he continued to waver between Jewish conservatism and Christian freedom, so Paul once rebuked Peter for his vacillation (Gal. 2:11-14). We are encouraged to believe that truth eventually gained the victory, giving Peter the liberty that all believers should enjoy. When that day came, who would be more eager than this man to tell the world the good news that P. P. Bliss has put in our song books, "Free from the law, O happy condition"?

A Choice of Words
Matthew 15:21-28

Southerners of the American sort have an advantage, even over the English, when reading the King James Version. An Elizabethan vocabulary that has become a part of history in its native country has been remarkably preserved in parts of Dixie. Words such as *holpen* and *fetch* present no problems there. Southerners also feel quite comfortable with the apostle Paul's frequent use of *you all.*

A word from their own regional vocabulary may aid understanding of our Lord's encounter with the Syrophenician woman. The word is *hush puppy*. As a Gentile, moreover a descendant of the tribes that had originally inhabited Canaan, the woman knew that in Jewish eyes she was "a dog." The term was used abusively and expressed a harsh racial prejudice. Had Jesus used this term, the woman would not have been too surprised. He was, after all, a Jew. Real surprise arose from the fact that he used another word of softer, kinder implication. She knew that she was dealing with a friend when He avoided naming her for a canine street scavenger and likened her instead to a household pet.

Tasty cornmeal dough morsels that were given to domestic animals to quieten their yelping and yapping came to be called *hush puppies.* Today, no fried catfish meal is complete without them. What began as dog food are now restaurant delicacies. In our Bible story, the "crumbs" which a believing Gentile woman begged from the hands of Christ led to the blessing of a beloved daughter, making her healed and restored. How much can turn on a word! Since "out of the abundance of the heart the mouth speaketh" (Matt. 12:34), it is always Christlike, when faced with alternatives, to speak in ways that help and heal.

Miracles Unlimited
Matthew 15:30-38

In Old Testament times, Syrian King Ben-hadad's men rationalized over their defeat by Ahab, king of Israel, in these words, "Their gods are gods of the hills; therefore they were stronger than we; but let us fight against them in the plain, and surely we shall be stronger than they" (1 Kings 20:23). The false concept of territorial deities, only able to function within their own limited areas, was entertained by pagan nations and not unknown in Israel. The gods of the hills might win battles in the mountains, but would prove helpless in the valleys.

As representative of His Father, the Lord Jesus worked His miracles to relieve sickness, disablement, and hunger wherever need existed, regardless of place or race. The crowds who followed Him from "the coasts of Tyre and Sidon" (v. 21) were healed so wondrously that, though Gentiles, "they glorified the God of Israel" (v. 31). In Christ, the grace of God broke through physical and national boundaries to bring relief to stricken people, wherever they might be.

On the east side of Jordan, not far from the scene of the feeding of the five thousand, Jesus repeated the miracle, but this time in the Gentile territory of Decapolis. First five thousand Galileans, and then four thousand persons of mixed racial background were fed from the hands of the Son of God. His compassion embraced all people without regard to skin tone, language, or ancestry. His demonstrated power, whether to heal or to feed, foreshadowed the coming of His gospel that was to prove itself "the power of God unto salvation to every one that believeth; to the Jew first, and also to the Greek" (Rom. 1:16).

Insensitive and Hypersensitive
Matthew 16:1-12

The effective grouping of his materials was one of Matthew's skills. Here, by relating events in which Pharisees, Sadducees, and our Lord's disciples played major parts, he confronts us with the question: What did these normally polarized persons have in common? The answer: failure to perceive for themselves the significance of the miracles Jesus wrought.

That strange coalition of religious aristocrats revealed this by their insensitivity. Apparently, it meant little to them that the blind received their sight, the lame walked, lepers were cleansed, the deaf made to hear, and the dead raised up. These things, in their estimation, had no messianic values. They demanded the sensational and spectacular: wonders in the heavens, the sun turned to darkness, and the moon to blood. The Master's reaction was perhaps more eloquent in what He did than what He said, for it is recorded that "he left them, and departed." He walked away from professed religious men who could not recognize heaven's touch in the blessings that came to the handicapped and disadvantages among them.

But, sadly enough, His disciples also proved unresponsive to Jesus' mighty works. Embarrassed by their own forgetfulness, for they had brought no provisions for the day, they interpreted a reference to leaven as a rebuke of their mistake. In their hypersensitiveness, they were deaf to what their Master said and needed to be reminded that He who had twice fed thousands could handle the small matter of an overlooked lunch basket. To think on this might save me from needless fretfulness this very day.

trust more; think long-term, bigger, far sighted

Lord Above All
Matthew 16:13-20

From a cave in the foothills of Mount Hermon flows a stream that eventually becomes the River Jordan. That cave, which one traveler described as "a very sanctuary of waters," became a shrine to the gods in Canaanite times. Baal was worshiped there, then Pan to whom the Greeks dedicated the site, and finally Augustus, first of the Roman emperors to be regarded as a god.

To this place of confused loyalties Jesus led His disciples. In those days the shrine had become a city, raised to honor the great Caesar and, at the same time, immortalize its builder, Philip the Tetrarch. Praise and politics were intermingled at Caesarea Philippi. Superstition, adulation, and self-esteem all had their monuments there.

Against such a background the Master asked His penetrating question: "Whom say ye that I am?" (v. 15). But was the background so exceptional? The choice has always been between false gods, conflicting loyalties, personal ambitions, and the claims of God. For Peter, who was later to say to Jesus, "Behold, we have forsaken all, and followed thee" (Matt. 19:27), Caesarea Philippi provided the challenge to a great affirmation. In the presence of the ghosts of a dead paganism and the awesome prospect of a growing cult of emperor worship, he made his great profession of faith. "Thou art the Christ, the Son of the living God" (v. 16). Some thirty years later, he was to be tempted to save his life by joining ecstatic crowds in shouting, "Caesar is Lord!" But his loyalty had already been firmly resolved. He was Christ's man, in life and death. In a world that tests our loyalty every day, our commitment to Christ should be equally effective in giving us courage to stand our ground in faithful witness.

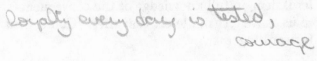

loyalty every day is tested, courage.

Price of Victory
Matthew 16:21-28

Early in 1940, to quote Winston Churchill's own words, "The slowly gathered, long pent-up fury of the storm broke." Holland, Belgium, and France fell before Hitler's advancing armies. Remnants of the British forces would make their escape through Dunkirk. On May 15 the French premier was to report to Churchill, "We have been defeated. We are beaten: we have lost the battle." Two days before, the British leader had delivered his famous speech to the House of Commons in which he said, "I have nothing to offer but blood, toil, tears, and sweat." But he continued, "What is our aim? I can answer in one word: Victory— victory at all costs, victory in spite of all terror; victory, however long and hard the road may be; for without victory, there is no survival. . . . Come, then, let us go forward together."

For the Lord Jesus Christ the bottom line, too, was victory. He foresaw His coronation when "the Son of man shall come in the glory of his Father with his angels" (v. 27). But He had no delusions concerning the price of victory. For Him it meant rejection and death; for each of His followers, willingness to "take up his cross" on the assurance that "whosoever will lose his life for my sake shall find it" (vv. 24-25). Master and servant alike were given the prospect of future glory as inducement to heroic self-denial for the sake of others.

No true leader ever conceals the cost of high endeavor or the sacrifices that must be made ere right can triumph over wrong. The flesh shrinks from such heavy demands being always ready to cry out with Peter, "This shall not be" (v. 22). But the greatest leader of all time sets His face toward Jerusalem, in full knowledge of the consequences, and says to us as we face our lesser Calvaries, "Come, then, let us go forward together."

courage

Wide-Awake Saints

Luke 9:28-36

The great Spurgeon was always surprising his congregations with unexpected approaches to great themes. Once when he preached on our Lord's transfiguration, Spurgeon majored on Luke's statement concerning the disciples that it was "when they were awake" that they saw their Master in His resplendent glory together with those Old Testament worthies, Moses and Elijah.

Several years ago, a young Japanese musician was rewarded for his progress by a gift from his father of a trip to a European capital and a ticket to a concert by a world-famous violinist. On arriving at his destination, the young man was captivated by everything he saw and wore himself out seeing the sights of that historic city. When he eventually went to bed he slept so heavily that, on awakening the next day, he discovered that the concert he had come to attend was over. By indulging his curiosity and expending his energies unwisely, he missed what he had traveled thousands of miles to hear.

The weariness of the twelve could probably be explained. But the fact remains that by yielding to a physical demand, they nearly missed what proved to be one of the spiritual high points of their lives. Sleepy-eyed discipleship can be a threat to any Christian's experience. To be too tired to pray suggests a poor sense of priorities, for this may shut the door on potential blessing. To be too tired to read God's Word, to go to church, or to engage in any spiritually rewarding activity indicates the need for a change of life-style so the best may be realized. Because God is at work in His world, we need to stay awake lest we miss some mighty evidence of His presence and power.

Handicapped Healers

Mark 9:14-29

Two letters that crossed in the mail started Florence Nightingale on her nursing career as "Lady of the Lamp." One was written by Miss Nightingale herself to the wife of a member of Parliament, offering her services as a nurse in the Crimea. The other was from the husband of the woman suggesting she go at government expense. Both writers were acting in defiance of Victorian conservatism that stood as a barrier between wounded and dying men and women willing to minister to them. Whether it was "proper" or not for a cultured lady to become a nurse, Florence Nightingale was determined to respond to a cry of need.

Inability to respond to need of any kind must always cause concern to persons of goodwill. Yet how often our desire to help is neutralized by our lack of ability! There are situations, of course, in which we share no blame for inaction. But the Master's censure of His disciples is a sharp reminder that opportunity to serve may sometimes pass us by because of our spiritual unreadiness.

When our Lord first came on the scene at the foot of the mountain, He found His disciples and the scribes engaged in a battle of words. There was "a large crowd around them and some teachers of the Law arguing with them" (v. 14, GNB). When religious debate is marked by animosity it can always be counted on to draw a crowd. World media never fail to pay attention when the church fights, either within its own ranks, or with others. The pity is that, as long as words fly, the redemptive ministry for which we exist not only goes unfulfilled but is called into question. Only when the Lord's people are involved in communication with the Lord Himself can we have the prospect of useful service.

Fifteenth of the Month
Matthew 17:22-27

Matthew had once been a tax collector. Is it surprising, then, that he alone among the Gospel writers recorded this fascinating incident about Jesus and the Temple tax? Every male Jew of twenty years and above was expected to pay it. Around the first day of the month Adar (March), notice was given that the tax would be due on the fifteenth. Collecting stations were then set up in principal cities, even beyond Palestine where Jews formed a considerable part of the population. There would have been one at Capernaum.

Perhaps it was for the benefit of those Jews of the dispersion that Matthew preserved this story. Nobody likes paying taxes, and distance from the Temple would seem to provide a good reason for not contributing to its support. Jesus could have pleaded His divine sonship as exempting Him from this obligation. But He sought no relief, even though to raise the money He had to send Peter fishing. There are duties that everyone owes and from which no Christian should claim exemption.

The apostle Paul's exhortation, "Wherefore come out from among them, and be ye separate, saith the Lord" (2 Cor. 6:17) is one of the more abused texts of the New Testament. It has encouraged in some an otherworldliness that has been practiced at the expense of life's common responsibilities. The same apostle told believers in Rome to pay "taxes to whom taxes are due, revenue to whom revenue" (Rom. 13:7,RSV). So world evangelist D. L. Moody was nearer the New Testament pattern when he said, "My citizenship is in heaven, but I pay my taxes in Cook County, Illinois."

Child Care
Matthew 18:1-14

George Bernard Shaw is quoted as having said of himself, "In my teens I was a professed atheist." If blame can be attached to anyone for this youthful unbelief, Shaw's father must bear some responsibility. This man maintained the practice of family prayers until his son was about ten years old. He would often read Bible stories aloud for young George's edification. But having done so, he would sometimes hurl the Book across the room exclaiming, "It's all a pack of . . . lies!"

Some cultures venerate old age. The Bible sees society's highest values in its boys and girls. Instructions found in its early pages were given to adults to ensure that each new generation was exposed to the lessons of history and the basic truths of revealed religion. No Jewish child could enter his home or go about life's daily routine without being confronted by visual reminders of the faith of his fathers. Happy the Timothys of whom it could be said, "From a child thou hast known the holy scriptures, which are able to make thee wise unto salvation through faith which is in Christ Jesus" (2 Tim. 3:15)!

What is the prospect of spiritual stability for the latch-key children of America? Bumper stickers that ask, "Have you hugged your child today?" arouse the suspicion not only that many boys and girls go unhugged, but also miss the priceless advantage of parental example and influence so essential for molding good character and behavior. For the tragic fact is that a young life may suffer as much ill effect from indifference and neglect as from deliberate abuse. We may need another spiritual revival to change social patterns that are denying our children the very company of their parents and privileges that are legitimately theirs.

The Ticking Bomb
Matthew 18:15-22

In April, 1983, a crew dredging the River Thames brought up an unexploded World War II aerial bomb. After forty years that bomb was still ticking and, therefore, a potential source of destruction and death. A bomb disposal squad had to be summoned to defuse it. Only then could it be handled with safety.

An unforgiving spirit is capable of exploding with harmful consequences long after the occasion that sired its anger. When Klaus Barbie was returned from Bolivia to France to face trial for wartime atrocities, forty years had passed since those crimes were committed. Neither time nor distance could deter his enemies from hunting him down and bringing him back to the scene of his enormities.

If any voices were raised in protest at this, they were not clearly heard. Even the most Christian conscience can apparently justify long-drawn-out anger against a human monster. Fortunately, as C. S. Lewis has pointed out, our practice of forgiveness is not normally related to extreme cases such as this. We can test the depth of our Christianity in our attitude to people who have annoyed or hurt us in the narrower circle of the home, the church, or the workplace.

Are we sufficiently in tune with the Spirit of our Master that we will extend forgiveness until we have lost count? That was the challenge given to Peter. And, had our Lord so desired, He could have offered the example of the Heavenly Father whose patience with repeated transgressions is one of the marvels of human experience. We don't have to be sons of Jacob to be included in this declaration, "I am the Lord, I change not; therefore ye sons of Jacob are not consumed" (Mal. 3:6).

Talents and Trifles

Matthew 18:23-35

Having read our Lord's story, maybe we will think twice before we again pray, "Forgive us our trespasses, as we forgive those who trespass against us" (see Matt. 6:12). If so, His purpose will have been realized. For the Master treated His disciples to what a modern newspaper reporter might term "a dramatic story with lurid details" in order to make them understand that a forgiving spirit is an essential ingredient for a Christian character.

When the United States Senate was once discussing astronomical budget figures, the late Senator Everett Dirksen sarcastically remarked, "Soon we'll be talking about real money." For the times in which he lived, our Lord's reference to "ten thousand talents" was real money (v. 24). A person with only a thousand talents was the equivalent of a millionaire. For some unstated reason, a fabulously wealthy king had entrusted one of his officials with this huge sum. When he could not produce the money, the king ordered him and his family to be sold into slavery. Earnest pleading caused this autocratic monarch to relent. But when he learned that the official whom he had treated so generously had thrown another man into prison for defaulting on a trifling debt, his mood violently changed, and he handed the big debtor over to be tortured.

God is not like that heavy-handed Oriental tyrant, and Jesus never intended that we should draw this parallel. But God, even the God and Father of our Lord Jesus Christ, can react in indignation and judgment when those who have been beneficiaries of His mercy act without mercy toward others. For if true of anything, it should certainly be true of forgiveness, "Freely ye have received, freely give" (Matt. 10:8).

History's Unhappy Harvests
Luke 9:51-56

Enmity between Jews and Samaritans was centuries old. It had its focus in Jerusalem's Temple, for the rebuilding of which Samaritan aid was refused. "Ye have nothing to do with us to build an house unto our God" (Ezra 4:3) was the sharp rebuff. So, eventually, Samaritans built their own temple on Mount Gerizim and vented their anger on generations of Jewish pilgrims bound for Jerusalem's annual feasts.

When our Master became the victim of this prejudice, James and John were anxious to prove that when it came to intolerance, they could outdo the Samaritans any day. They appealed to the Old Testament for a precedent to their proposed act of fiery retaliation. How convenient to the mood they were in that it was in the vicinity of the city of Samaria where Elijah called down fire from heaven to destroy two bands of fifty sent to arrest him (2 Kings 1:9-12)!

No prize for Bible knowledge was awarded the Sons of Thunder that day. Instead, Jesus rebuked James and John for misrepresenting the Spirit of the Son of man who had come not "to destroy men's lives, but to save them" (v. 56). By the same token, He issued an implied warning against claiming scriptural support for unchristian attitudes and actions. To resort to violence in the name of Christ is to negate every principle of love and kindness that Jesus both exemplified and taught. Even an expression of hatred against persons who raise barriers to Christian advance in the world is a betrayal of our Master's spirit. We must learn to disagree without being disagreeable, to recognize opposition and error without excoriating those who practice it. Otherwise, we shall go on sowing and reaping history's unhappy harvests.

Protected Privilege
Luke 9:57-62

When, in years to come, the church life of this century is honestly evaluated, one of our gravest mistakes may be recognized as the ease with which persons were admitted into membership. Zeal for statistical progress has encouraged great laxity in procedures for adding names to our church rolls. Seldom are persons who walk the aisles in response to post-sermon invitations confronted with the seriousness of what they are doing or the continuing obligations imposed by Christian discipleship.

To be among the knights of the Round Table was the dream of chivalrous youth in King Arthur's day. But conditions of admission to that select circle were strenuous. It is said that when stalwart young men were exposed to the initiation tests, they emerged from them pale and trembling. The honor of a place among the heroes of Camelot was given a high price, and none but a select few qualified.

Salvation's door is open wide "to every one that believeth" (Rom. 1:16). But the quality of belief was obviously a matter of concern to the most zealous preachers of the gospel. When the Ethiopian eunuch asked for baptism, Philip the evangelist replied, "If thou believest *with all thine heart,* thou mayest" (Acts 8:37, author's italics). There was no place then in the ranks of the redeemed for the half-hearted, any more than there should be now. Our Lord set the standard of fellowship so high that He has been criticized for harshness. But in the light of His own complete commitment —He had just reaffirmed this as "he stedfastly set his face to go to Jerusalem" (Luke 9:51)—had He not every right to demand undivided loyalty from those who aspired to walk in His steps?

(See *Day by Day with John,* pages 44-58.)

Gossipping the Gospel
Luke 10:1-16

When, in the fourteenth century, John Wycliffe sent out his itinerant preachers, he must have consciously instructed and equipped them on the pattern set by the Lord Jesus when He commissioned the seventy. Wycliffe's men went barefoot, without purse, and with a staff in their hands. At one point in his struggle against the established clergy, he had so effectively made his opposition known that, in his words, "it was discussed in the streets where every sparrow twittered about it." When he took open measures to give the Bible to the people, his enemies complained that "the gospel pearl is cast abroad and trodden underfoot of swine."

Those whom Jesus dispatched were sent "into every city and place, whither he himself would come" (v. 1). They were His advance men, preparing all whom they met for the day when they would be face-to-face with Jesus Himself. They were the messengers of an approaching confrontation, so critical for those who experienced it that it would issue in divine judgment. Sodom and Gomorrah would fare better at the final assize than those cities of Galilee that rejected the heralds of the kingdom and its gracious King.

The situation is similar today. He who came on foot to Chorazin and Capernaum will one day return to this earth in the clouds of heaven, and "every eye shall see him" (Rev. 1:7). When He spoke of that future event, He said that before it would come, "this gospel of the kingdom shall be preached in all the world for a witness unto all nations" (Matt. 24:14). This, then, is our task, for God has ordained that by the spoken word the gospel shall be made known until Jesus comes again.

Give God the Glory
Luke 10:17-24

Without denying the seventy any of the joy they had earned from a task well-done, the Master brought them down from the dizzy and dangerous heights of recent success to the safer level of contemplating God's marvelous grace. More important than what we may do for God is what He has done for us. To dwell on the former is to run the risk of self-inflation. To think on the latter is to live in a spirit of unceasing wonder and gratitude.

One of the stranger characters of the New Testament was Simon Magus. The inspired record gives us insight into his character by telling us that he "bewitched" people by "giving out that himself was some great one" (Acts 8:9). His greed for prominence through the possession of supernatural power brought a severe rebuke from Peter, who told him, "Thy heart is not right in the sight of God" (v. 21). First in fact and later in popular imagination, this man haunted the Christian community for many generations. He has been named as the father of gnosticism, the heresy that bedeviled the churches in the early Christian centuries.

Basic to effective and acceptable discipleship is a humble and grateful spirit. We are not surprised that God was glorified in the life of one who wrote, "Unto me, who am less than the least of all saints, is this grace given, that I should preach among the Gentiles the unsearchable riches of Christ" (Eph. 3:8). This is the spirit of those whom Jesus described as "babes," distinguishing them from the self-evaluated "wise and prudent," and opening the door to significant service to all who know their weakness and look to Another for their strength.

The Heart Has Its Answer

Luke 10:25-37

These two men, the equivocating Jewish scribe and the compassionate Samaritan, need to be kept together. For it is in the contrast between these two and their behavior that a major lesson lies.

Lawyerlike, the first had come to Jesus primed for debate. He already knew the answer to his lead question, "Master, what shall I do to inherit eternal life?" (v. 25). He must have heard our Lord deal with others when they had raised this same matter, for he was quick to give the correct scriptural reply, earning the commendation, "Thou hast answered right" (v. 28). But then he revealed his real motive. In a second question, loaded with controversy, he asked, "And who is my neighbour?" (v. 29). This scribe, and others like him, were always ready to argue an issue about which they had already made up their minds.

Jesus provided no opportunity for discussion. Instead, he told the story of a man who found the answer to the scribe's question, not in debate but in action. A despised Samaritan provided both reproof and example to a paragon of religious orthodoxy because, instead of speculating about neighbors and neighborliness, he responded with compassion to a person in need. He saw an opportunity to serve, seized it, ministered to another human being without hesitation or inquiry, and became a pattern for all to follow. "Go," said Jesus, "and do thou likewise" (v. 37). In a period of religious rancor over church practices and beliefs, it is said that dissenting ministers of the English Episcopal order established themselves in popular favor when, in the Great Plague of 1665, they risked their lives in service to the dead and dying.

When Jesus Said No
Luke 10:38-42

Was the occasion for this intriguing incident the Feast of Tabernacles? Many authorities believe so, and to accept their suggestion is to possess an explanation why Martha was so busy playing the bountiful hostess. For, among the Jews, the Feast of Tabernacles was like Thanksgiving and Christmas rolled into one—a time of merriment and feasting, when any woman worth her salt put out her best effort to outdo her neighbors in splendid repasts.

Martha's idea for honoring her distinguished Guest was to provide Him the best meal her pantry would allow. And, had she maintained her cool, she might have been praised for doing so. But Martha got flustered. The sight of sister Mary sitting at Jesus' feet was too much for her. Luke helps us sense Martha's rising temperature by telling us that, to address Jesus, she "came to him" (v. 40), perhaps "came at Him." We can hear the rustle of her skirts as well as the annoyance in her voice. "Tell her to come and help me!" (GNB), she said. And Jesus answered no.

Of course, He was too gracious to respond with a sharp negative. But in well chosen words, He spoke warningly, not only to Martha but also to Luke's readers in the early churches, with a lingering message for us. For when we are so busy doing things for the Master that we have no time for quiet fellowship with Him, we are too busy. "Lord, if in the tasks of today I should fail to think of thee, think thou of me" has a cute sound, but it is poor Christianity. The "good part" that Mary chose is too precious to be bartered for any activity, however worthy in itself. Life's schedule must provide time for contact with our Lord if life's pathway is to be followed without stumbling.

Call Him Father
Luke 11:1-13

At the heart of our Lord's teaching on prayer is the fatherhood of God. From her experience as tutor to the crown prince of Japan, Elizabeth Gray Vining has told how, in the now-departed imperial days, members of the royal family lived apart from one another. The heir to the throne, though only twelve years old, was housed away from his parents as were his brother and four sisters. This unnatural separation, a carryover from the rigid conservatism of the past, prevented the development of normal family relationships, a tragic loss to all concerned.

God's sovereignty is no barrier to communication and fellowship between Him and His children. Early Hebrews were so awestruck by the name of God that they refrained from using it. Not surprisingly, they had little concept of the fatherhood of God. How amazed, then, the disciples must have been when they first heard their Master address His prayers to *Abba* (Father)! How much greater their surprise, and hopefully their delight, when He instructed them to use the same form of address! "When ye pray, say, Our Father" (v. 2). In speaking to the Almighty, they were to use the intimate term they had employed when talking to their earthly fathers.

But having said this, Jesus elevated the Heavenly Father above all earthly parentage which he described as "evil" though only to contrast human imperfections with the unsullied goodness of God (v. 13). In effect, He paid high tribute to this world's fatherhood by acknowledging its protective and providing care. We may take the considerate concern of our parents as encouragement in making our requests known to God. For to call Him Father is to recognize in Him all human compassion raised to an infinite degree.

The Finger of God
Luke 11:14-26

When plagues were visited on Egypt, the third of which Pharaoh's magicians were unable to imitate, they covered their confusion by saying, "This is the finger of God" (Ex. 8:19). An unwilling acknowledgement was forced from them that things were happening beyond their control or manipulation. By a touch of His finger, the God whom the Hebrews worshiped had proved His superiority over all the deities of Egypt.

Challenged by His critics to account for His healing power, our Lord attributed His miracles to "the finger of God" (v. 20). He who had reached out to punish a nation for holding His people in cruel bondage reached out again in Christ to deliver those who were in direr bondage to Satan. No rallying of the armies of heaven was needed in either case, no mustering of the forces that made the universe. The power that flowed through God's finger was enough to bring about a nation's deliverance or break the shackles of a tormented mind.

According to Jesus, the wonders wrought in His ministry by God's finger were evidence of the approach of the heavenly kingdom. What of God's power and splendor has been revealed in part will one day be fully manifested in the completion of His purpose to bring all things under His sovereign control. Eventually, for the ultimate revelation and establishment of His kingdom, He must unleash that awesome power by which the worlds were made. It shall then be acknowledged that "his right hand, and his holy arm, hath gotten him the victory" (Ps. 98:1). But for now, in the exercise of both justice and mercy, we see the activity of "the finger of God" and never more clearly than in the ministry of Jesus who "went about doing good" (Acts 10:38).

Let Light Shine
Luke 11:27-36

When visiting an Eastern penitentiary, in the course of his praiseworthy prison ministry, Charles Colson was confronted by a convict who asked, "Remember me?" The man told how, in another jail, Colson had found him in a dark cell in which the light fixture had been long broken. A visit to the warden took care of the problem, so this inmate was able to say with evident gratitude, "You gave me the light." The chaplain of the institution told Mr. Colson that the man had subsequently decided to follow Christ. He had assumed that nobody cared for him until this unexpected friend came along and gave him the gift of light.

By its very nature, light affirms that it is meant to be shared. Any amateur photographer who has tried to construct a darkroom knows the difficulty of excluding light. It has an irrepressible determination to invade any area of darkness to brighten it by its presence. God made light that way. Give it a pinhole and it will become a beam. Give it a crack and it will do battle with darkness, so there is no doubt as to who will win. Light is as unconfinable as love, ever breaking forth where it is most needed to remind us of the persistent grace of its Creator.

Startling indeed is the warning Jesus gave against being full of darkness. Clearly, this dread possibility is the result of how we look at things, for the eye is either the window through which light enters, or the barrier by which light is excluded. Our Lord had presented Himself as "a greater than Solomon . . . a greater than Jonas" (vv. 31-32). Do we see Him in His true stature as Son of God and Light of the world? If we do, His light will fill and overflow our beings.

An Unfamiliar Role
Luke 11:42-54

In the last book of the Bible, there is a phrase so paradoxical that it startles the reader. The people of the earth, great and small, are said to hide themselves from "the wrath of the Lamb" (Rev. 6:16). Since the figure of a lamb obviously refers to our Lord's redemptive mission, the association of wrath with One who is generally recognized for His gentleness and mercy evokes surprise.

"If the Redeemer, that appeases the wrath of God, Himself be our wrathful enemy," wrote Matthew Henry, "where shall we have a friend to plead for us?" It surely behooves us to know what occasions His anger, to know what offenses cause the very incarnation of divine grace to exchange His normal role for words and deeds of reprimand and retribution.

Pride and hypocrisy accounted for the woes that Jesus pronounced upon these scribes and Pharisees. These two sins—for sins they are—become cause for stern rebuke throughout the Scriptures. They go hand in glove, for when a person thinks too highly of himself he invariably resorts to pretense to magnify his virtues and conceal his faults. When exposed, as they were by Jesus, pride and hypocrisy lead to other sins—desire for vengeance that finds ultimate expression in violence.

Pride and hypocrisy turned persons in Jesus' time into His bitter enemies. The troublesome thought is that these were highly religious people about whom the Master pronounced His woes. Could it be that the twin evils that stirred His anger then are present threats to Christian character and conduct?

Feathered Teachers
Luke 12:1-12

Blind men, introduced to an elephant for the first time, had widely different impressions. One took hold of the elephant's trunk and decided that the animal was like a snake. Another felt the legs and said an elephant must be similar to a tree. A third grasped the tail and could imagine nothing other than a rope.

We can be grateful to Luke for bringing together a selection of sayings of our Lord for they enable us to form well-rounded opinions about His teaching. They even set important truths in contrast as when, in one verse, Jesus said, "Fear him," and two verses later, "Fear not" (vv. 5-7). In both statements He was speaking about God, in the first case as divine Judge and the other as compassionate Creator. He addressed His listeners as "my friends" (v. 4), indicating that He was speaking to their advantage by confronting them with two opposite sides to the nature of His Heavenly Father.

Though we may flinch from the word *fear*, it is so firmly written into the inspired record that it merits careful consideration. By the time this Gospel was written, Christians had been exposed to persecution by the state. Fear of the ruthlessness of enemies, the anguish of imprisonment, torture, or even death might cause them to waver in faith, if not deny it. For them, the fear of God needed to take priority over fear of men who, at worst, could only kill the body while God has jurisdiction over body and soul. But what if the worst was realized and faithfulness brought death? Of that dread possibility Jesus said, "Fear not," for He who has set high value on the life of a sparrow sets higher value still on the eternal welfare of His redeemed children.

Wealth Without Wisdom
Luke 12:13-21

Millions watched on television as he was carried from plane to ambulance, then to a hospital to die. Reputed to be one of the wealthiest persons in the world, he had accumulated money as some men shovel dirt. Life's experiences had been tasted to the full, but none gave him satisfaction or lasting enjoyment. Labeled an eccentric, he deteriorated into an international recluse, shifting constantly from location to location, breeding rumors about himself that kept the gossipmongers busy. The final glimpse of him revealed a shriveled body, hollow eyes, unkempt hair, and telltale features of one who for all his wealth was to die in utter loneliness.

Rich persons whose lives end in tragic anticlimax have a strange fascination. We may be sure that the story told by our Lord about "a certain rich man" (v. 16) grabbed and held the attention of His hearers. But they should also have paid heed to the man in the crowd whose request prompted this story. For we may not all be rich, but most of us would like to be, and that puts us in the company of him who said, "Master, speak to my brother, that he divide the inheritance with me" (v. 13).

While Jesus was talking about solemn aspects of discipleship, this man's mind had been on the money he could not get. Christ's significant words meant nothing to him for he was preoccupied with desire for an inheritance that, for some reason, had evaded him. With all heaven offering him its blessings, all he could ask for was help to get his hands on the family fortune. Did he not deserve to be called fool, as much as the man in the story, for allowing the prospect of material gain to close his mind against God's greater good?

Did He Mean Me?
Luke 12:35-48

Interruptions were neither uncommon nor unwelcome in the teaching ministry of our Lord. A lawyer, made uncomfortable by what Jesus was saying, broke in to say, "Thou reproachest us also" (11:45). A member of His audience, ignoring the substance of His teaching, spoke up asking Jesus to speak to his brother about a disputed inheritance. And now, here is Peter intruding with a question, "Lord, does this parable apply to us, or do you mean it for everyone?" (12:41, GNB).

To illustrate the need for preparedness in life and particularly in relation to His own return, Jesus had described servants awaiting the arrival of their newly married master and a householder's need to be on constant watch against thieves. He added the pointed comment, "Be ye therefore ready also" (v. 40). Perhaps Peter heard an unfriendly voice say, "See, He doesn't even trust you!" So, to cover the embarrassment of himself and the other disciples Peter gave Jesus an opportunity to explain that He was speaking to all present, not just to a few.

But the Master did not respond as Peter had hoped. He continued His parabolic method, making increasingly clear that He was directing his words to persons like Peter to whom had been given special responsibilities. The disciples were obviously those to whom "much is given," and of them, therefore, "shall be much required" (v. 48). When the Word of God appears to us to become too personal, a natural reaction is to broaden its application so that its impact is distributed more widely. In a congregation of people, this ruse is most effective. But when we are alone in the presence of the Lord and His penetrating Word, it is good that we face up to the fact that this means me!

Fire that Divides
Luke 12:49-59

The story of Patrick, evangelist to pagan Ireland, abounds in legends—some of positive value, others less so. Among the more worthwhile is one which tells how he answered fire with fire. When kings and druids were once gathered in the palace of Tara waiting for the falling of the sacred fire, all other lights having been extinguished in superstitious reverence; on the horizon a flame was seen. King Laeghaire sent chariots, horsemen, and foot soldiers to see who was responsible for this sacrilege. They found Patrick worshiping, with others, before a rough altar on which burned the offending light. The Christian group was seized and taken to Tara. As they went, they sang, "Some trust in chariots, and some in horses; but we will remember the name of the Lord our God." Patrick's words before the assembled dignitaries subdued their opposition. Before many years, the power of paganism in Ireland was broken.

Of Christ's coming into the world it was said, "the light shineth in darkness" (John 1:5). On His own statement, the shining light was also a dividing fire. As Patrick's flame challenged the superstitious fires of Tara, so the fire that is Christ has challenged the false fires of philosophy and religion and demanded of persons that they declare their allegiance. He never concealed that to do this would bring controversy and conflict with consequent rifts even within families. For persons blessed with memories of "the family pew," symbolic of shared faith with all its attending joys, the reminder is sometimes necessary that, in many places, the divisions of which Jesus spoke are harsh realities. How richly blessed are those whose homes are united in devotion to the Master! How deserving of our prayers are all who, for His dear sake, endure the sorrow of family opposition!

Payday One Day
Luke 13:1-9

Quisling was the name of a Norwegian diplomat. But because of his collaboration with the Nazis in World War II, his name came to stand for "traitor" in any language. Few people are more despised than those who sell themselves to the enemy of their country.

Perhaps the men who worked on the tower of Siloam fell into this category. They may have been building fortifications for the Romans. As such, they were perfect examples for the point Jesus was making. He had been questioned about some Galileans whom Pilate slew in the act of offering their sacrifices. These men would have been popular with the majority of their fellow countrymen. The builders at Siloam, on the other hand, would have been highly unpopular. Yet both groups met with disaster. Did this prove, Jesus was asked concerning the Galileans, that they were sinners above all others, visited by God with punishment suited to their offenses?

The strong, repeated negative of our Lord's reply was intended to correct the idea, prevalent even among His disciples, that suffering is evidence of sin. Disaster should be a warning to all, He said, of coming judgment, but not interpreted at the personal level as a sign of divine displeasure. Yet many Christians still labor under the false assumption that life's misfortunes can be traced back to some moral or spiritual offense for which God is exacting payment. All sin will ultimately face its consequences unless pardoned for the Savior's sake. But pain and tragedy in the believer's present experience are used in the mysterious processes by which our Heavenly Father seeks to fashion character, develop sympathy for others, and draw us nearer to Himself.

Satan's Nemesis
Luke 13:10-21

Without attempting to probe related theological complexities, it can be observed that, in the record of this miracle, pathetic physical conditions were attributed not to God but to Satan. It was God who, in the person of His Son, freed the woman from her eighteen-year bondage. It was He, too, who, in spite of the woman's extreme deformity (she was bent double), declared her still to be "a daughter of Abraham" (v. 16). Let others conclude from her infirmity that it is punishment for past transgression. Jesus affirmed her full status as a member of God's covenant people.

The occasion was one of our Lord's last visits to a synagogue. A circle of hatred was closing in on Him, making it increasingly dangerous for Him to enter situations that were controlled by His enemies. Yet He not only attended this synagogue but challenged prevailing traditions by healing on the sabbath day. The motivation of pity must be given full recognition. It was not possible for divine love to encounter human need without a response of compassion. But we should also recognize the determination of the Master, whatever the risks involved, to confront prejudice and hypocrisy and make a stand for mercy and truth.

His embarrassed adversaries probably told themselves that the end was near for this troublesome prophet from Galilee. But by parables of mustard seed and leaven, Jesus declared not an end but a beginning. For by message and ministry the gospel of relief and redemption would extend its influence throughout the world, until the works of Satan will be finally destroyed and the kingdom of God will universally prevail.

(See *Day by Day with John,* pages 59-60.)

Lament for a City
Luke 13:22-35

The prophet Jonah took a hillside seat overlooking ancient Nineveh, hoping against hope that he might see that city destroyed. Prussian general Blucher, seeing London for the first time, displayed the worst side of military genius when he exclaimed, "What a city to sack!" But Jesus viewed Jerusalem through tear-dimmed eyes as He thought of its lost opportunities and approaching doom.

He had that same day been asked a question, "Lord, are there few that be saved?" (v. 23). How could his mind avoid going back to Abraham's day and that patriarch's plea for Sodom? Would God spare the city for fifty righteous people? For forty-five? For forty? For thirty? For twenty? For ten? Not as many righteous persons could be found as could be counted on the fingers of two hands.

Among the sad things our Lord said that day was that some who thought they qualified as righteous were self-deceived. Because they had rubbed shoulders with Jesus "We have eaten and drunk in thy presence, and thou hast taught in our streets," (v. 26), they assumed that they had contracted Christianity. But faith is not caught like the measles. It is possessed by conscious and deliberate response to the gospel and by sincere commitment to Him of whom it tells. Right there is the need for evangelism in town and country, but particularly in cities, that people everywhere may hear the life-giving words and have opportunity to open hearts and minds to them. Why particularly cities? Because those best qualified to know tell us that urban communities are being largely overlooked in our programs of evangelism. Surely, the apostle Paul knew what he was about when by both spoken and written word he addressed his message to cities.

Four-Letter Words
Luke 14:1-14

A child had been lost in the Cumberland Mountains. A search had continued for several days, on the ground and from the air. But no success had attended these efforts. A succession of cold nights had lessened the probability that the boy was alive. So the search had been abandoned—by all but the boy's mother. She would go on looking, she said, so long as her strength held out. The lost child was, after all, her son.

When Jesus questioned fellow guests in the chief Pharisee's home, he may have said, "a son or an ox" (v.5, GNB). Both son and ass are four-letter words in Greek, so alike in appearance as to be easily confused. There is good manuscript evidence for believing that the Master said "son," and this probability provides food for thought. In essence Jesus said, "Look at this sick man. If he were your son, would you be more inclined to bend the rules?"

In all three conversational cameos preserved by Luke—the sabbath issue, the place-conscious guest, and the supper invitation—He was exposing the trait of self-interest. His reason was clear: self-interest, whatever it may have to commend it, often exists at the expense of others. A beloved child will be rescued, even on the sabbath, though a sick stranger must go unhealed. A prominent seat will be grabbed at a feast, regardless of the displacement of someone else. A guest list will be drawn up to flatter the host's own ego while hungry people go neglected and unfed. Parental response to a child in jeopardy is both natural and commendable. But this concern should foster, rather than exclude, the recognition of cases of need in the larger human family, and the acceptance of responsibility for children of misfortune.

RSVP
Luke 14:15-24

An invitation to supper at a friend's house is one thing. An invitation a "a great feast," presumably at a palace (in Matt. 22:2 the host is a king), is entirely something else. We may wriggle out of an unwanted engagement at Tom, Dick, or Harry's. But what if the occasion is a meal with someone at the top of the social ladder? What if the invitation comes from God?

Jesus had in mind something better than a royal feast for His parable was given in response to a table companion's pious remark, "Blessed is he that shall eat bread in the kingdom of God" (v. 15). He warned the speaker of this shallow comment by describing a festive event from which guests excused themselves by claiming business and domestic priorities.

When VIPs extend their hospitality, you don't say no. One of the angriest scenes in the Old Testament occurred when David was absent from King Saul's table. Jonathan received a verbal clobbering because his friend offered a made-up reason for deserting the royal table (1 Sam. 20:30-31). Yet the call to the gospel feast is ignored by multitudes. And even those who call God "Father" are adept at finding reasons for not appearing in the house where He dispenses spiritual food.

The shocking part of our Lord's parable is concerned with the substitute guests. Jesus was warning His Jewish listeners of the penalty of neglect and of the Gentile guests who would take their places at heaven's table. But we do ourselves service by acknowledging our own danger of allowing material and social interests to rob us of the sublime blessings that come from setting high value on every opportunity for feasting with God.

Folly of the Underestimated
Luke 14:25-35

No war in this century has been the occasion of more controversy and political fallout than that in Vietnam. Withdrawal short of victory was a severe blow to our national pride. One salutary result was a firm resolve not to enter again into a foreign military commitment with uncertain consequences. A mistake once made is a forceful argument for sitting down and counting the cost of any future engagement.

Jesus was comprehensive in His condemnation of the folly of embarking on projects without clear understanding of everything involved. He pictured an individual, probably a farmer, contemplating the construction of a tower. Then He spoke of a nation assessing its chances of victory in war. In both cases, His counsel was the same: Don't begin anything without estimating the expense involved and thus making ready to finish it.

Jesus was speaking of discipleship. Then as now, people were eager to declare themselves His followers without giving due consideration to the cost. One of these costs could be a rift in family relationships as the claims of Christ came into conflict with established traditions. A person could be forced into the unhappy situation of having to determine his primary and lesser loyalties, who came first in his life and who must stand aside that God's will might be done. Converts from Islam who see their parents in street procession behind an empty coffin understands what it means to hate (love less) their own kinfolk that Christ may have the preeminence. Such an extreme separation may not be asked of us. But every day we face issues that test our willingness to go all the way with Jesus, regardless of the consequences.

Losers and Finders
Luke 15:1-10

The point of Lincoln's Gettysburg address is gained, or missed, according to where we put the emphases—not on the prepositions *of, by,* and *for,* but on *people.* His plea was for preservation of "government of the *people,* by the *people,* for the *people."*

The appeal of a lost sheep and a lost coin must not blind us to the fact that Jesus, through His parables, was talking to people about people—to murmuring Pharisees and scribes about a faithful shepherd and a determined housewife whose conduct reproved indifference toward the lost. True, the sheep and the coin were lost, and because of this the shepherd and the woman were threatened with being losers. They could have remained losers. But by resolute action, they became finders. They experienced all the joy that comes from recovering things that are precious. They turned losing into finding.

The Master would have us know that God turned losing into finding. The earnestness of His campaign to win back those who stray is expressed in such Old Testament statements as, "I have spread out my hands all the day unto a rebellious people" (Isa. 65:2), and, "I have spoken unto you, rising early and speaking" (Jer. 25:3). But the supreme evidence of His concern for the willful and wayward was the coming into this world of "our Lord Jesus, that great shepherd of the sheep" (Heb. 13:20), who described His mission to be "to seek and to save that which was lost" (Luke 19:10). To do this Jesus consorted with "publicans and sinners." This was an offense to some spiritually complacent religious leaders of His time. But to those who know their true condition and need, the revelation of a God who will stop at nothing to snatch the perishing from disaster is occasion for deep amazement and heartfelt gratitude.

A Father's Son
Luke 15:11-24

W. Hay Aitken was a dignitary of the Church of England and as effective an evangelist as his generation produced. His call to evangelism came through the ministry of that great American layman, Dwight L. Moody. Night after night, even on Saturday, Canon Aiken would preach on the prodigal son. He would come down from the pulpit into the aisles, in earnest appeal to his listeners to make their peace with God. The drama of a seeking Father was reenacted in the preacher's method, so that our Lord's story of a wayward young man never failed to bring other wanderers home with the confession, "I have sinned against heaven, and in thy sight" (v. 21).

The plight of our Lord's prodigal is vividly described by the hunger that led to a depraved appetite and loneliness unrelieved by the simplest kindness. But what of the anguish of the father, left at home, waiting, wondering, and worrying? The father's tragedy is repeated 100,000 times a year in America today, for that is the appalling number of missing children reported to the police. In some states, a program of fingerprinting youngsters has been started as a means of tracing any who might disappear. The deepest impression, surely, is on the hearts of parents whose loved ones vanish, sometimes never to return.

But the prodigal did return to a glorious welcome by a father overjoyed to see his son once more. Strangely, in telling this happy conclusion our Lord did not say, as He did of the recovered sheep and coin, "Likewise, . . . there is joy in the presence of the angels of God" (v. 10). Perhaps he did not need to, for we clearly see the forgiving and restoring grace of our Heavenly Father in the reception of the boy who came home.

The Prodigal Who Stayed at Home

Luke 15:25-32

To become a prodigal it is not necessary to leave home. The older son at his best was as far away from the spirit of his father as the younger at his worst. Both boys made it necessary for the father to go out from his home to deal with them. But the younger was escorted into the house with a loving arm around him. His sour-faced brother apparently stayed outside, pouting and glowering because of imagined injustices.

The many verses that separate the opening and ending of this chapter should not cause us to forget that it began and concluded with hostility, Taking their stand on the pedestal of their own self-righteousness, a group of the hyperorthodox had taken Jesus to task for engaging in table fellowship with some so-called undesirables.

The attitude of the older brother was only an element in a story, but it mirrored the real-life ugliness of those whose only reaction to people they despised was to shun them. Jesus would have had them know that by condemning Him they were condemning God, whose love pursues the most unlovely and will not rest until it has redeemed and restored.

That divine love shines through the conduct of "a certain man" who "had two sons." He had words of welcome for the delinquent boy and nothing but sweet reasonableness for the disgruntled one. "My boy," said the father, "you are always with me, and everything I have is yours" (v. 31, NEB). But conciliation did not work. It seldom does when people allow the green-eyed monster to embitter their lives.

How to Win Friends
Luke 16:1-13

Jesus' true humanity is seen in his capacity for humor. While all that He said had weight and wisdom, Jesus did not abstain from popular appeal but added interest to His words by the skillful use of arresting phrases and apt illustrations. His reference to a person with a log in his eye (see Luke 6:41) is an example of the former, while this story of the crafty steward has proved its attention-getting quality by the controversy it has aroused since it was first told.

Unfortunately, the Gospel writers had no way of capturing the expression on our Lord's face or the tone of his voice when He talked to His changing audiences. He was a careful observer of life and saw the good and the bad going on around Him. Jesus did not hesitate to draw on both to give a point to His messages. Jesus did not approve the steward's dishonesty but placed him among "the children of this world." Jesus did hold up this man's astuteness and enterprize as challenges to His followers to show equal zeal and initiative in the business of God's kingdom.

The steward's method was dishonest in the extreme and not to be excused because he may have learned his dishonesty from his master. But the man's objective was to win friends, and Jesus endorsed that by telling His disciples they needed to do the same. They could use their possessions, however little or much they might have, to gain for themselves a circle of eternal friendship in "everlasting habitations." To reach heaven and be greeted by those who say "I am here because of you" will mean happiness without end.

Beggar with a Name
Luke 16:19-31

In no other parable told by Jesus is a character given a name. The rich man is nameless, but the beggar is called Lazarus, "one whom God helps." By adopting a name for the rich man, Christian tradition has subscribed to the idea that wealth must have recognition. Anyone "clothed in purple and fine linen," who also "fared sumptuously every day" (v. 19), deserved a handle. So Dives, the Latin word for "rich," was conferred on him to save this affluent character from anonymity.

Thus a purpose of the great Storyteller has been obscured. Did the owner of the big house at whose gate the beggar was laid daily ever give him a name? Whether he even noticed the poor wretch is in doubt; and, if he did, was it not with feelings of revulsion? The beggar belonged to the nameless, faceless multitudes of this earth who daily go hungry while the rest of us eat our fill. Many are the people of the so-called Third World, a term that thrusts them beyond the horizons of our responsibility. In these desperate days, however, they may not necessarily be in other continents but, like Lazarus, at our very doors. Was it not Jesus who said, "For ye have the poor always with you" (Matt. 26:11)?

In the Scriptures the bestowment of a name is of great significance, for Bible names relate to status, reputation, and character. That our Lord should name the beggar revealed His regard for the lowly, underprivileged persons of this world. He was saying that, according to the principles of His kingdom, everybody is somebody. The nameless ones are those who, regardless of their social standing, live selfishly and without concern for the suffering around them. They leave this life with nothing except regrets and excuses. The future, the eternal future, belongs to those who, knowing their need, seek and find help in God.

Labor of Love
Luke 17:1-10

Although our Lord's invitation to "all ye that labour and are heavy laden" contained the promise "I will give you rest," it also included references to "my yoke" which implied discipline and "my burden," conveying responsibility (Matt. 11:28-30). His teaching on discipleship was far removed from the gospel of an easygoing life that is sounded from many quarters today. There were times, in fact, when He could have been considered harsh in His statement of the obligations of the believer.

Faced by His demands for exemplary living and a forgiving spirit, His disciples exclaimed, "Lord, Increase our faith," (v. 5). They felt that they did not have enough of what it takes to maintain so high a level of behavior. His reply was that the effectiveness of faith does not depend on quantity but quality. When faith is real it can achieve the impossible, enabling erstwhile spiritual weaklings to leave no stumbling blocks in the way of others but, on the contrary, to provide uplifting examples by patient, forbearing attitudes toward all who offend against them.

Forgiveness must have been a frequent theme in our Lord's teaching. He gave it a prominent place in His pattern prayer for disciples. On one occasion, Peter sought commendation for His suggestion that the reasonable limit for overlooking offenses was seven times. The response of "seventy times seven" must have staggered him (Matt. 18:21). But disciples must learn that, when they have gone the limit in any duty, and beyond, they are still "unprofitable servants." When this is the estimate of ourselves and our service, when, in fact, we evaluate everything we do for God and others in light of what He has done for us, then the surprise will await us of His "Well done, thou good and faithful servant" (Matt. 25:21).

(See *Day by Day with John,* pages 61-64.)

Odd Man Out
Luke 17:11-19

Social caste systems have a way of breaking down under the pressure of crisis. People who avoid one another in normal conditions bury their discriminations when faced by common disasters. Unfortunately, however, these periods of mutual tolerance are usually short-lived. Return to normalcy too often brings a recovery of old distinctions and divisions. This was noticeably so in Europe in World War II. Princes and paupers fought, suffered, and died side by side. But with the conclusion of hostilities, society again began to separate into the haves and have-nots.

The ten lepers were an unusual group, for among them was one who was obviously odd man out. Nine of them were Jews and the tenth a Samaritan, though it was truthfully said that "the Jews have no dealings with the Samaritans" (John 4:9). Racial and religious prejudices had apparently yielded to the shared tragedy of leprosy, for the cure of which all ten sought the help of Jesus. The faith of all ten was put to the test when the Master told them to act as healed men, to go and show themselves to their priests.

Why did the Samaritan turn back to pay his tribute and praise to God in Christ? We cannot be sure, but it is possible that, with healing, came a reassertion of anti-Samaritan sentiment. The alien in the group was made again to feel ostracized and alone. To whom could he turn but to the One who had healed his body's hurt and could be trusted to give relief to his aching heart? In giving praise, he himself was praised, for few things are more pleasing to God and persons than gratitude.

Blind to the Signs
Luke 17:20-37

When, in AD 79, Vesuvius erupted and buried Pompeii in its fiery lava, one tenth of the population of 20,000 perished. Signs of approaching disaster had been around for some sixteen years but had been ignored. Bodies recovered from the terrible embalming of volcanic deposits give evidence that people were going about life's normal routines when the end came. They were living for today and tomorrow in total unawareness that, for them, tomorrows had run out.

Preoccupation with the future, at the expense of the present, is not a new phenomenon. In Jesus' day, rabbis and others calculated and speculated on prophetic passages of the Bible much as sensation mongers do today. But when a group of Pharisees wanted Jesus to join in this game, He refused. The kingdom of God, He said, does not come "by looking for signs of it" (v. 21, Phillips). His questioners were straining their eyes peering into the distance and entirely missing the fact that the Kingdom was already present in Jesus Himself.

A stinging statement in the Book of Proverbs affirms that "the eyes of a fool are in the ends of the earth" (17:24). The reproof is for persons whose gaze is so fixed on the horizons of time that they are unaware of important happenings around them. In the mixing pot that is modern Israel, there are small radical groups that refuse to cooperate with the government while they concentrate all their attention on the coming of the Messiah. For these, and others like them, it is sadly true that God's kingdom will not come "by looking for signs of it." The Messiah for whom they wait has already come, and the call of the gospel to Jew and Gentile alike is to believe in Him.

Parables and Parallels
Luke 18:1-14

Neither the judge nor the widow had anything to commend them. The man, appointed to uphold the law, debased it by his corrupt practices. The woman who petitioned the law proved herself a vixen. She harrassed the judge until he became fearful for his life—"lest at the last she coming strangle me" was the way Wycliffe gave real meaning to "lest by her continual coming she weary me." He was a rascal and she a shrew!

There is no portrayal of God here, nor yet of the believer at prayer. The purpose of the story was to establish contrasts. God is not unjust or unfeeling but much the opposite; therefore, those who approach Him need not fear they will be ignored nor resort to extreme practices to get His attention. His answers may not come by return mail, but come they will, so that the most hard-pressed believer may have confidence in relief. That our Lord should wonder whether at His return He would find this kind of faith still in evidence may expose a growing prayerlessness among Christian people.

With the skill of a writer who had a deep understanding of what he was writing, Luke paired one parable with another. The Pharisee and the publican are vastly different characters from the judge and the widow. The Pharisee was respected for his piety and revealed in his reputation. He even thought that God should hold him in high regard for his exceptional goodness. The publican had no delusions about himself and asked only for mercy. When Hugo Grotius, reputed founder of international law was dying, a friend seeking to counsel and comfort, mentioned this second parable to which Grotius responded, "I am that publican."

Resort to Controversy
Matthew 19:1-12

The southward route taken by our Lord on leaving Galilee and crossing into Perea, or "Judaea beyond Jordan" (v. 1), would bring him to Jerusalem in time for the Passover: in time, too, for betrayal and death. Those who would bear the major responsibility for His coming crucifixion dogged His footsteps as He journeyed, ever watchful for opportunity to embarrass and accuse Him.

Divorce was as controversial a subject then as it is today. In Perea, it was loaded with both political and theological overtones. Herod Antipas, who ruled the territory, had recently divorced his wife to marry Herodias, taking her from his half brother. Criticism of this immoral relationship had already cost John the Baptist his head. Would Jesus allow His enemies to draw Him into perilous comment? Would he take sides in a dispute that had Jewish theologians in opposite camps, the one liberal and the other legalistic?

Our Lord did not dodge the issue, and He did take sides. He stood pat on the creative intentions of His Father and on the permanence of the marriage bond. Even the disciples shied away from the concept of a partnership with no loophole for escape. Would it not be better to remain single? The culture to which they belonged, though basically religious, had liberalized their thinking, for it permitted the sacrifice of women to the whims of men. It could even plead Moses as authority for its law divorce practices. For Jesus, the only authority for morality in human relationships was God Himself. In Christian circles, where compromise and accommodation also exist, should not Jesus' stand for the preservation of family unity be our sought-after ideal?

Friend of Children
Mark 10:13-16

Set a person in the company of children, and you may learn more about his character in ten minutes than might be otherwise possible in a year. The Blair family of Silver Spring, Maryland, cherished the memory of a visit to their home by President Lincoln. He played with the grandchildren on the lawn where he ran around like one of them, except that his black coat-tails were flying in the wind. Lincoln's own children were always special to him so that, no matter how important the occasion, they were always free to demand his attention and be swept up into his arms. His office was a refuge for little ones in trouble, either from their mother or an angered servant.

The disciples were guilty of nothing worse than trying to protect their Master from what they regarded as unreasonable requests. But their concept of childhood was wrong, and Jesus straightened out their warped thinking with the plainest of words. He did not need to be protected from children whom He recognized as potential citizens of His Father's kingdom. It was, and is the children who need protection and never more than now.

What a sad reflection on our civilization that child abuse and molestation have in recent years become a national issue! Yet, when all has been said and done in efforts to save boys and girls from physical neglect and moral danger, the greatest disservice possible remains largely unrecognized. To keep them, by whatever means or reason, from the presence of Christ is to deprive them of blessings immeasurable. Jesus is still saying to all who have the charge of children, "Suffer the little ones to come unto me, and forbid them not."

Robbed by Riches

Matthew 19:16-22

Some people think of wealth as the golden key that will open any door. How mistaken they are! As many of this world's rich have discovered, one door it will not open is happiness. Neither can money provide an entrance into eternity's coveted bliss.

Atahualpa, the last king of the Incas, tried to buy off the Spaniards and so save his life. "If I cover this floor with gold and silver," he said to the conqueror, Pizarro, "will you set me free?" The room measured seventeen by twenty-two feet, and Pizarro was incredulous. But the Inca stuck to his offer. Drawing a red line on the wall, as high as he could reach, he promised to furnish gold enough to reach to that mark and silver sufficient twice to fill an adjoining room. But when the Spaniard saw all the gold and silver, he wanted more and more. Finally, Pizarro accused the Inca of plotting against the invaders and had him put to death in the plaza at what is now Cajamarca, Peru.

The rich young ruler was so wedded to his wealth that he would not part with it even to gain that eternal life that he professed to desire. Had he listened more carefully to our Lord's gracious invitation, "and come and follow me" (v. 21), he could have found release from the tyranny of worldly possessions and so gained that greater boon he so eagerly sought.

There is not enough money in the world to buy salvation, but there is enough money in many a person's pocket to keep him from it. No story has a sadder conclusion than this encounter between a man of wealth and the Savior, for it is written that "he went away sorrowful: for he had great possessions" (v. 22).

Possible Impossibilities
Matthew 19:23-30

Often the impossibilities of life are the phantoms of our own false reasoning. The disciples provide an example. They clung to the notion that was as old as Job, that life's desirable things are the rewards of virtue. A rich person's prosperity was to them, therefore, a sign of divine approval. Their neat theory was dealt an unexpected blow by the *verily* of emphasis with which Jesus introduced the statement, "That a rich man shall hardly enter into the kingdom of heaven" (v. 23). If the gateway to paradise does not readily swing open at the approach of the affluent, what is the chance for admission to a poorer person?

The camel and the needle's eye added to the dismay of the Master's listeners as He doubtless intended they should. For His desire was to advance their thoughts from imagined impossibilities to real ones. Could any greater impossibility be envisioned than that a motley group of ex-fishermen and ex-tax gatherers should "sit upon twelve thrones, judging the twelve tribes of Israel"? (v. 28). Yet He held out that unlikely prospect to reinforce His claim that "with God all things are possible" (v. 26).

Bernard W. Spilman, pioneer Sunday school worker and founder of the Ridgecrest Baptist Conference Center, deleted the word *failure* from his dictionary. He had enough problems to threaten failure to his endeavors, but he believed so strongly in his call to be a Christian educator that, with God's help, he turned impossibilities first into possibilities, then into actualities. Beginning with his own salvation, every believer, whether rich or poor, may experience the triumph of accomplishment in matters which with men are impossible but not with God.

"Who Follows in His Train?"

Mark 10:32-45

The most common ecumenical experience for most Christians is when they open their hymnbooks to join in the worship of God. Our songs of testimony and praise are written by persons from all sections of Christendom, and somehow their compositions make perfect harmony with seldom a discordant note.

A specially rich contribution to universal hymnody was made by an Anglican clergyman, Reginald Heber. Best known of his hymns are "Holy, Holy, Holy, Lord God Almighty," "From Greenland's Icy Mountains," and "The Son of God Goes Forth to War" with its recurring questions: "Who follows in His train?" Heber's own selfless service in the gospel affirmed his willingness to follow, whatever the cost. Turning his back on comfortable and influential office at home, he accepted a pioneer missionary post in India where he died after three years of unsparing toil. His farewell sermon, on leaving his homeland, was on the words, "For ye are dead, and your life is hid with Christ in God" (Col. 3:3).

Jesus strode resolutely along the road to Jerusalem causing amazement, and even fear, among those in His company. After He had again foretold His death in that city two disciples, still dreaming of a messianic kingdom with Jesus at its head, asked for political favors. In their minds, they dissociated themselves from the redemptive mission of the Master that they might satisfy their selfish desires. Like them, we too often shrink from identification with a crucified Savior that we may pander to our preferences and ambitions. Heber's question challenges our self-serving substitutes for loyal discipleship. "Who follows in His train?"

Gift of Inner Vision

Mark 10:46-52

When He reached Jericho, our Lord was eighteen miles from Jerusalem. There in a matter of hours, He would ride into the city, greeted by emotional crowds that would cry, "Hosanna to the son of David: Blessed is he that cometh in the name of the Lord" (Matt. 21:9). Those tributes of praise were anticipated, however, by a blind beggar who, possibly with deeper sincerity than the Palm Sunday crowd, also addressed Jesus by a messianic title, "Son of David." Who can say which was more meaningful to our Lord, the chorus of voices that awaited him in Jerusalem or the plaintive cry of Bartimaeus of Jericho, "Jesus, thou Son of David, have mercy on me" (v. 47)?

Blindness has its compensations. The ear is often keener, the sense of touch more alert, the mind more perceptive, and the heart more responsive. This beggar who halted our Lord's progress toward the Holy City had never seen the One to whom He appealed. Yet He believed in Jesus' power to heal, saluted Him in terms of the expected Messiah, persisted in his purpose against the chiding of the crowd, knew his need, boldly made request for healing and, being granted the boon he sought, abandoned his beggar's bowl and "followed Jesus in the way" (v. 52).

But it is not always so. John Milton did not submit uncomplainingly to his visual handicap. He complained to God, "Thou revisit'st not these eyes, that roll in vain to find thy piercing ray, and find no dawn." But though no natural light blessed his sightless orbs, the world is debtor still to that spiritual vision which enabled him to "assert Eternal Providence and justify the ways of God to men." Some are healed that, Bartimaeus-like, they may be witnesses to his mercy. Others are sent uncured onto life's battlefield that, in their victories, they may give daily testimony to God's power.

The Sinner's Guest
Luke 19:1-10

One was looking for a friendly face, the other for a quiet lodging. They met on a street crowded with pilgrims bound for Jerusalem. One was up a tree, seeking a place of vantage from which to see the man called Jesus of Nazareth. The other—Jesus Himself—was in the mass of humanity below, where angry voices denounced the stubby tax gatherer as he clung to a swaying branch. Then in a passing moment, the needs of both were met. In a voice whose warmth contrasted with the abuse that flowed from the lips of others, Jesus said, "Zacchaeus, make haste, and come down," and swiftly added, "for to-day I must abide at thy house" (v. 5).

Imagine what it must have been like to bear a name that meant "the righteous one" and yet possess the reputation of being the biggest scoundrel in town! Until that day, such had been the unhappy lot of Zacchaeus. He could not join the pilgrim company passing through Jericho, for he was welcome neither in synagogue nor Temple. But he could at least watch and wish, recalling those better days before he sold out to the Romans when he, too, celebrated Passover with family and friends. His special hope was to catch a glimpse of Him about whom it was whispered that he might be Israel's promised Messiah.

Little did Zacchaeus realize that Jesus, too, had a need or that he would be called on to supply it. That, however, is the way the divine plan of redemption works. The greater benefactor is always the Lord, for He can bring friendship and forgiveness to forlorn lives. But the receiver of such blessings is not without means of response. Zacchaeus opened his home and his heart, as should we, to this gracious Guest. "If any man hear my voice, and open the door, I will come in to him, and will sup with him, and he with me" (Rev. 3:20).

False Expectations
Luke 19:11-27

Messianic fervor never reached greater heights than at the approach of the annual Jewish feasts. The Temple was firmly linked to the fulfillment of the promise of the coming of a national deliverer. If the purpose of God required that He should "suddenly come to his temple" (Mal. 3:1), when better than on one of those occasions when the nation was assembled representatively in Jerusalem to commemorate past deliverences and so to celebrate God's final vindication of His earthly people?

Such thoughts occupied the minds of those who accompanied our Lord along the last few miles between Jericho and the Holy City. Knowing their thoughts, Jesus felt the need to disabuse their minds "because he was nigh to Jerusalem, and because they thought that the kingdom of God should immediately appear" (v. 11). His parable of the pounds was intended to correct false expectations by putting an unstated interval between that moment of misguided popular enthusiasm and His eventual accession to His kingdom. During that uncertain interval, His followers must prove their faithfulness in the midst of a society that rejected both His claims and His person. "We will not have this man to reign over us" (v. 14) is the perennial protest of the unbelieving world.

The soon-departing nobleman, for so Jesus described Himself, would give each of His followers the same assignment, a "pound" of responsibility for bearing witness to the gospel in an unfriendly environment. The sad thing for Him and for us is that the best He could expect was that two out of every three would prove worthy of His trust. The defaulter (God grant that I am not he) would identify more with Christ's enemies than His friends until he adopted the language of rebellion and deprived himself of the reward of loyalty.

107

Day of the Donkey
Matthew 21:1-11

Three hundred years before Christ, a young Greek general engaged in a campaign of conquest that molded the Eastern world into one vast empire. His name was Alexander the Great, acclaimed by some as the offspring of a god and by others as a god in his own right. His chain of victories included Palestine and proceeded eastward as far as India. The world trembled at the name of Alexander whose fame was enhanced by the reputation of his steed Bucephalus, a horse so magnificent and terrible that none other would dare to ride or even touch him.

Toward the end of his three-year ministry, the Lord Jesus made what is often called His "triumphal entry" into Jerusalem. That esteemed scholar, William Hersey Davis, objected to the term. To him, it identified our Lord's action with the self-glorifying victory parades of earthly conquerors. There was both studied humility and peaceful intention in the ride that our Master so carefully planned. He mimicked no war-intoxicated victor but took His cue from an ancient prophecy about a King: "just, and having salvation; lowly, and riding upon an ass" (Zech. 9:9). To Dr. Davis, this was a "royal entry," made by one who had a rightful claim to the throne of His people but would unsheath no sword to obtain it. He was the Prince of peace, content to tread a painful road that "all wreaths of empire" might eventually be His through the outworking of His Father's redemptive purpose.

Both Alexander and Jesus died at about the same age. But whereas Alexander's empire has long since ceased to exist, Christ's kingdom looks forward to its most glorious hour when "The kingdoms of this world are become the kingdoms of our Lord, and of his Christ" (Rev. 11:15).

Goodness and Severity
Matthew 21:12-22

The contrasts are sharply drawn. Compare Matthew, if you will, with an artist who makes his thunderclouds more intense by displaying them against the golden rays of the sun or the dramatist who alternates his scenes so that the darker moods of his characters are made more striking by emphasis on their gentler moments. To His disciples, Jesus must have seemed unpredictable as they witnessed His acts of indignation and His deeds of compassion, sometimes following one another in quick succession.

Today, this Master of ours would be condemned by many as a spiritual leader who betrayed His mission to become a political activist. Granted there were Temple abuses that needed correcting, but was it consistent with His redemptive ministry for Him to cleanse the sacred courts of those who exploited them for personal gain? Unfruitfulness, in a tree or a nation, was a grievous condition; but should this Advocate of love and peace have spoken the words of judgment that withered the tree and warned the nation?

As the Father's Son, Jesus could do no other than reflect the divine disposition to both "goodness and severity," to use the apostle's phrase (Rom. 11:22). We do Him grave disservice by depicting Him as a passive observer of life—crying "Peace! Peace!" when there is no peace—and allowing evil to take its course without protest or resistance. We may gladly focus on the gentleness of His nature as He healed the sick and commended little children for their hosannas. But not to shift the focus to those sterner moments when He assumed the role of judge is to overlook the profound biblical concept of "the wrath of the Lamb" (Rev. 6:16). The Psalter describes our right response when it exhorts; "Do homage to him truly, lest he be angry, . . . happy are all who shelter beside him." (Ps. 2:12, Moffatt).

(See *Day by Day with John,* pages 67-69.)

Questioning Questioners
Luke 20:1-8

When, in 1775, Ethan Allen and his Vermont volunteers, the Green Mountain Boys, appeared before Fort Ticonderoga demanding its surrender, the surprised British commander asked for Allen's authority. Surprise must have turned to amazement at the brash reply, "In the name of the great Jehovah and the Continental Congress!"

There was nothing evasive in that answer with its blend of religion and politics. Neither did our Lord avoid the issue when He answered a question with another question. In fact, He was using a method of the scribes themselves whereby truth could hopefully be brought into the open. Was authority the subject? Then let the critics express themselves concerning the authority of John the Baptist. If they accepted his credentials, then they must reckon with his witness to Jesus. If they denied them, they must answer to the crowds whose fervor for the Baptist had never waned.

Both theology and politics were active ingredients in the encounter in Jerusalem. As the Master clearly perceived, the purpose of His questioners was to involve Him in a statement that could be labeled either blasphemous or seditious. Instead of falling into their trap, He confronted them, in a reversal of roles, with a manifestation of His God-given authority. Those who assembled as the interrogators were met with the imperious demand, "I will also ask you one thing; and answer me" (v. 3). He made that bold demand of friends and enemies alike as when, having described Himself as resurrection and life, He asked of Martha, "Believest thou this?" (John 11:26). And that imperative question put to the Twelve—"Whom say ye that I am?" (Matt. 16:15)—lingers in all our ears as the Master's test of every Christian's loyalty. "Answer me!"

God Forbid!

Luke 20:9-19

There were two exclamatory phrases in the language of the New Testament that could be (and one is) translated, "God forbid." Peter used one at Caesarea Philippi when he reacted to our Lord's announcement of his coming rejection and death (Matt. 16:22). The other appears in this so-called "parable of the wicked husbandmen," actually much more than a parable. The fate of those who abused the owner's messengers and slew his son was so incredibly shocking to Christ's listeners that they exclaimed, "God forbid" (v. 16). Thus people express their objection to things they would rather not hear and close their ears to words that upset their self-serving concept of the future order of events.

Our Lord's extraordinary survey of Jewish history, given in terms of a vineyard, its owner, and the conduct of those entrusted with its care, confronts us with two dangers. We may allow our system of prophetic interpretation to take the sting out of what was intended as a grave warning to a rebellious people. Or we may restrict a lesson on the consequences of betraying a solemn trust to those who heard it that day in Jerusalem's Temple, and miss its wider application that includes ourselves.

Over a dozen times, the apostle Paul, in his epistles, paused to write the words, "God forbid." This was his reaction to the serious implications of things that he believed and taught. "Hath God cast away his people?" he asked concerning Israel, and added, "God forbid." The thought was agony for him. But so also was the dire prospect that awaited disobedient Christians. Hence his warning that "if God spared not the natural branches, take heed lest he also spare not thee" (Rom. 11:1,21). His "God forbid" was not an escape from reality but a summons to face unpleasant truth and react accordingly.

111

Pocket Change
Matthew 22:15-22

When our Lord was still a child living in Nazareth, Judas of Galilee led a revolt against paying taxes to Rome (Acts 5:37). The rebellion was ruthlessly crushed by the Romans. But the issue raised by this patriot lived on, not only as a political grievance but more particularly for religious reasons. The tax was a constant reminder of Jewish subjugation to Rome. The coin used to pay the tax was an affront to the biblical concept of only one God. For on the coin was the inscription, "Emperor Tiberius, August Son of the August God."

The Master's strategy in asking His questioners to produce one of these coins, presumably from their own pockets, was designed to expose their hypocrisy. When Pontius Pilate had recently assumed authority in Palestine, one of his early acts outraged the Jews. Ignoring the restraint of his predecessors, he ordered Roman military standards which bore the likeness of the "divine" emperor into the Temple area. The reaction was so violent that even Pilate was forced to back down. Yet those who so successfully protested what to them was sacrilege, accommodated themselves to carrying about and using currency that should have been equally offensive to their religious susceptibilities. To serve their own advantages, they were willing to sacrifice their principles. As Jesus so pointedly charged, they were hypocrites.

Perhaps we should not condemn them too readily. For which of us has not, in some way or other, surrendered convictions to expediency? For us to "Render . . . unto God the things that are God's" (v. 21) must surely mean that we will commit ourselves to a consistency of belief and practice that will not retreat before the threats of others or our own self-interest. Hypocrite is an ugly word in any language.

Refuge of Controversy
Matthew 22:23-33

There is an often-told story of a preacher who wrote in the margin of his sermon manuscript, "Shout here. Argument weak." Persons who assume unreasonable positions are likely to resort to cheap tactics to save their faces. These Sadducees are a fair example. They thought to embarrass our Lord with a ludicrous proposition that had probably been the frequent cause of shallow merriment in their own discussions.

No severer judgment could be passed on religious leaders than for them to be told, "Ye do err, not knowing the scriptures, or the power of God" (v. 29). Yet ignorance of the inspired Book, or perverse misinterpretation of its teaching, is the root cause of all heresy. It is splendid to know the content of the Bible, but not enough. We must earnestly seek to understand what it says, setting aside preconceived ideas and prejudices, and following reliable teachers—chief of whom are the Lord Jesus Himself and the Holy Spirit.

Among other things, we must mold our thinking about the world to come on the pronouncements of the Scriptures. Some would envisage heaven as a glorified earth where life continues much as it is now, though on a higher plane. The revealed truth is that God's redeemed people will experience a transformed existence in a timeless spiritual realm whose realities are beyond our mortal grasp. In the absence of any contrary statement we must believe that present relationships, though greatly changed, will in some fashion survive. That great Scottish preacher, Arthur J. Gossip, dedicated one of his books, "To my wife, my daily comrade still, with gratitude, and love, and hope." After her death, he inscribed another book, "To my wife, now a long time in the Father's house." In life, or death, "gratitude, and love, and hope" survived.

The Mind and the Master
Mark 12:28-37

By admitting that, "Into each life some rain must fall," Longfellow allowed for sunny intervals. In the providence of God, rain and sun together achieve His purpose for our lives. Was it not so with Jesus? As the satanic design that would accomplish His death became more brazenly evident, and the voices of His enemies grew louder and harsher, there were also signs of acceptance to assure Him that His suffering would not be in vain.

Out of the ranks of the mostly critical scribes there stepped a man with an honest question. He had been listening to what the Master said, not to cause mischief but to learn. And believing that Jesus had an answer that would satisfy both mind and heart, he asked, "Which is the first commandment of all?" (v. 28). After receiving the reply he added his own endorsement to what Jesus had said, and for this earned a warm commendation for his sincerity and perceptiveness.

In this context, we must not miss the significance of the addition of "with all thy mind" (v. 30) to our Lord's Old Testament quotation or the scribe's matching phrase, "with all the understanding" (v. 33). Together they give importance to this incident for its emphasis on spiritual intelligence as an essential part of Christian devotion. While our Lord often used picture language to appeal to His hearers, He never talked in trifles. His messages were addressed to mind and heart, as when He discussed the status of the Christ as "Son of David" (v. 35). This was tough teaching, yet it is pointedly stated that "the common people heard him gladly" (v. 37). Today, as then, the critical need of humanity cries out for truth that heals the worst as it challenges the best in every person.

When Little is Much
Mark 12:38-44

When religious leaders strutted their stuff in market-places, synagogues, and at social events that were open to the public, the crowds responded with servile admiration. One lonely voice was raised in warning that outward demonstrations of piety may conceal calloused hearts and hypocritical intentions. Conspicuous giving to the Temple treasury was part of the act. The trumpet-shaped receptacles, into which offerings were cast, lent themselves to public displays of generosity that were rewarded with shallow praise. But Jesus said, "Beware" (v. 38). He saw through the dramatized religiosity of these people and reserved His commendation for a widow's "two mites, which make a farthing" (v. 42). Such a gift, for all its smallness, was great in His eyes.

Participants in a broadcast quiz program successfully identified a number of prominent individuals from activities in which they had recently engaged. Politicians, military personnel, and authors were among those recognized and named. But then came a question that stumped the panel. Who was the person who decided that rather than wait for his estate to be divided after his death, he would make the distribution in life? Who was it that called together representives of sixteen charities and made handsome gifts to each? Nobody knew. The largeheartedness of a citizen of Cleveland, Ohio, had gone unnoticed by competitors who were playing for their own financial gain.

The God who "loveth a cheerful giver" (v. 7) takes note of and correctly evaluates every good deed. He is not so much interested in the amount as in the motive and spirit of our giving. Millions or mites are equally pleasing to Him when they are given, not of compulsion nor pride, but in willingness and love.

Edifice Complex
Mark 13:1-10

In February, 1934, fire did serious damage to the meeting place of the First Baptist Church, Nashville, Tennessee. The pastor of the church then, Dr. W. F. Powell, used to tell how he talked with a man who was wringing his hands and wiping away his tears as he watched the smoke and flames. On being questioned, this man acknowledged he had never been inside to worship, but the sight of a building dedicated to the glory of God being destroyed had worked heavily on his emotions.

To an extent, all of us derive a sense of personal security from noble structures. Their presence, and daily visibility, gives assurance of stability in a world in which so much is uncertain and transient. This was so with our Lord's disciples. The magnificence of Herod's Temple never ceased to impress them. In a moment of unrestrained enthusiasm, they asked the Master to share in their pride, only to receive the crushing news that the day was coming when those sculptured stones would be overthrown, so "there shall not be left one stone upon another" (v. 2).

How solemn the thought that religious institutions and their material symbols will not escape the judgment that will accompany the coming of "the day of the Lord" (2 Pet. 3:10)! We have, in fact, an apostolic statement to the effect that "judgment must begin at the house of God" (1 Pet. 4:17). Not only will objects of our pride, though sacred in purpose, be submitted to God's evaluation and disposal, but every earthly expression of our spiritual aspiration must eventually give place to the more glorious realities of eternity. John's new Jerusalem had "no temple therein" because—and this should thrill our expectant hearts—"the Lord God Almighty and the Lamb are the temple of it" (Rev. 21:22).

Telling the Worst
Mark 13:11-20

Much of the influence of the late Winston Churchill can be attributed to his honesty with his listeners. When the outlook was dark, he did not offer soothing syrup but told the stark truth. His famous line—"I have nothing to offer but blood, toil, tears, and sweat"—was at the heart of his first speech as wartime prime minister.

A king of Judah once asked a prophet of God, "Is there any word from the Lord?" evidently hoping for a favorable response. The prophet's answer must have been devastating, "There is: for, . . . thou shalt be delivered into the hand of the king of Babylon" (Jer. 37:17). Did the thought cross the prophet's mind that a conciliatory statement might improve his standing with his royal questioner? If so, it was not allowed to affect his truthfulness as the mouthpiece of God. He stayed with the facts as they had been revealed to him, and though his utterance was of coming doom he honored his office and maintained his integrity.

On what ground do many of us suppose, as regrettably we do, that God's word to us must always be comforting and agreeable? There are modern-day prophets who pander to this expectation with a gospel overdosed with the saccharine of "God's in his heaven, all's right with the world." But there are surely times in life when we need to be shocked by a confrontation with reality. Those who serve us best are not necessarily persons who lull us to sleep with their soft and gentle tones but the less-welcome voices whose strident sounds jolt us into awareness of impending danger. If we listen attentively, even the most alarming pronouncements that come to us from God are tinged with mercy and, therefore, give cause for hope. Our Lord, most faithful of all God's spokesmen, promised the tempering of judgment for the sake of the elect.

Scattering and Gathering
Mark 13:21-27

Hiroshima and Nagasaki perished in a ghastly moment of atomic fury. But for Jerusalem the agony of death was prolonged. Secular historians have furnished the grim details culminating in destruction by the Romans in AD 70. Famine, internal strife, and Roman brutality contributed to a tragedy of overwhelming proportions. The Christian population escaped across Jordan before the final siege. Those Jews who remained and survived became a scattered people, deprived of both a national identity and a traditional home.

An event so catastrophic left its mark on Jews and Christians alike. For the former, hope was stimulated of restored power and prestige brought about by charismatic leadership which would achieve both political and military success. For the church, anticipation focused on a new Israel for whom God would prepare a new Jerusalem, a "holy city, . . . coming down from God out of heaven" (Rev. 21:2). Unfortunately, this Christian confidence became blurred by confusion concerning events that would precede this glorious climax to history.

This confusion was anticipated by our Lord in warnings and promises that not only caution against unwise speculation but also provide firm basis for believing in Him as the chosen agent of His Father's final plans for this world. Whatever the details of His glorious return, the grand strategy is plain. Over against the scatterings that have invariably followed history's grim conquests, there will be a glorious gathering together of God's elect, Jew and Gentile alike. Setting aside all debate about incidentals, we affirm with Paul that God has a purpose "which he set forth in Christ . . . a plan for the fulness of time, to unite all things in him" (Eph. 1:10, RSV).

Newspaper and Bible
Mark 13:28-37

The informed believer reads both his newspaper and his Bible. He is alert to what is happening around him and expectant toward future developments that have their place in the ultimate strategy of God. He interprets today's events with intelligence that is based on his knowledge of heaven's government of this universe. He looks with confidence to tomorrow, convinced of the unswerving purposes of God, and content to leave the scheduling of events to a higher wisdom. Concerning the final scenario, he is satisfied not so much to know as to watch.

As a corrective to those who have their eyes strained on the horizons of time and resist involvement with current happenings, our Master spoke in the same breath of both the immediate course and the coming climax of history. For His disciples, the signs of the times were related to events that would take place in "this generation," (v. 30). For their own good, and the benefit of those whom they might influence, His followers needed to be apt students of the prevailing scene. By acting on this counsel, many of our Lord's listeners escaped, and helped others to escape, the judgment that befell Jerusalem. Christians have a continuing duty toward their contemporaries. Necessarily, their message will be heavy with warning of the consequences of persistent sin, yet correspondingly strong concerning God's provision of a way of salvation in Christ.

What of the future? That, too, requires a positive attitude, for our Lord left no doubt about the certainty of His return. Our enthusiasm over this glorious prospect is both understandable and right. But should it not be tempered by our acceptance of the implied warning, so noticeably present in His second-coming pronouncements, that "ye know not when the time is"? (v. 33). Therefore, the summons is not to speculation but to watchfulness.

When Expectation Dies
Matthew 25:1-13

Don't blame the foolish virgins for going to sleep. After all, wise and foolish alike succumbed to the weariness of waiting. The great Storyteller Himself did not fault the ten bridesmaids at this point. He may, in fact, have mentioned their slumber as a needed reminder that life has to go on, both in waking and sleeping, while His coming is in abeyance. A feverish restlessness that can rob us, not only of sleep, but also of the capacity for sound reasoning is not an appropriate ingredient of Christian watchfulness.

The five young women whose lamps went out were unprepared for the apparent delay in the bridegroom's coming. The flames of their enthusiasm flickered and died as the unexpected hours went by. When at last the cry of welcome sounded, they were sadly unequipped to join others in the glad festivities. Neither could they rekindle their cold wicks with borrowed oil. The flame of enthusiasm will only burn in the fuel of personal dedication, effort, and preparedness.

Among first-century Christians for whom Matthew wrote his Gospel, unfulfilled expectations of our Lord's early return gave place to disbelief in some and discouragement in others. The apostle Peter tried to refuel the lamps of his contemporaries by echoing their own disgruntled question, "Where is the promise of His coming?" He responded to prevailing scepticism by affirming "the day of the Lord will come" (2 Pet. 3:4-10). Assumed delay was evidence of human ignorance of divine scheduling; and, in fact, if there is postponement in God's ordering of events, this is because of his mercy toward sinners to give them time for all to "come to repentance" (v. 9).

Pounds and Talents

Matthew 25:14-30

If there is a familiar ring about the parable of the talents, the reason is that our Lord used the same framework to provide two different lessons. In the parable of the pounds (Luke 19:11-27), He talked about responsibility. In the companion parable of the talents He dealt with ability. To every believer is entrusted the "pound" of the gospel, a sacred stewardship to be fulfilled by a dual witness of words and works. Discipleship imposes on all of us an obligation to trade wisely and well with "the treasure put into our charge" (2 Tim. 1:14, NEB), the saving knowledge of God in Christ.

How we go about this will depend on our abilities—our *talents*—for the translated word that Jesus used has passed into our vocabulary to define our God-given endowments. Unlike the "pound" which signifies an equal responsibility for all, the "talents" vary and, with their variations, have expectation of different levels of performance. Yet in a sense, the same obligation rests on the five-talent person as the one-talent person—faithfulness in service.

That internationally popular Bible teacher, G. Campbell Morgan, had four sons, all of them ordained ministers. On one occasion when all were together, a visitor asked the youngest who was the best preacher in the family. After a moment's hesitation during which he looked at each family member in turn, the young man replied, "Mother." The eloquence of the father had been handed down in lesser degree to his boys. At least two of them gained reputations as outstanding pulpiteers. But within the home circle, a unanimous opinion prevailed that by her encouragement of and intercessions for the more public ministries of husband and sons, Mrs. Morgan qualified as "a good and faithful servant" (v. 21).

Ultimate Authority
Matthew 25:31-46

Alexander the Great, at the peak of his career, is said to have wept when he learned from Anaxarchus of the existence of many worlds beyond our own. His tears expressed his regret that with other fields for military adventure, "we have not yet conquered one." Success turned sour for him because of possibilities of power that were beyond his grasp.

Amid a clamor of conflicting interpretations of our Lord's parable—Who, for example, are the "sheep" and who are the "goats"?—a different focus of attention may be suggested, namely, the speaker Himself. On the human level, the cause He had espoused for the past three years seemed doomed to failure. Even as He spoke, His enemies were completing their plot to bring about His death, aided by the treachery of one of His inner circle. He was fully aware of the direction events were taking. Had Jesus not told His disciples that betrayal, condemnation, and death awaited Him in Jerusalem (20:17-19)? Yet He shed no tears, either for Himself or for goals unrealized. On the contrary, He spoke as one who had the reins of authority in His hands: not as the victim of others' hate but as a mighty Victor who held the destinies of all within His power.

Our Master saw beyond the cross which, while an emblem of divine love, is also a monument to human cruelty and injustice. He saw Himself arrayed in kingly splendor, seated "upon the throne of his glory" (v. 31), possessed of universal authority and dispensing universal justice. By His edict, the inequities of this topsy-turvy world will be reversed. Eternal rewards will go to those who have shown compassion to others and everlasting penalties to the unkind and unmerciful. The qualities of the King will determine the nature of His kingdom.

A Sweet Savor
Mark 14:1-11

To many people, the advertising industry touches bottom ethically and aesthetically in its television promotion of perfumes, shampoos, and toiletries. The appeal of such advertising is sickeningly sensual as plastic-faced models scent their bodies, massage their skin, and flaunt their hair in poses and scenarios that provide a revolting commentary on our overindulgent culture. From the sophisticated beauty who tells us her product is expensive "but I'm worth it" to the suggestive verbal dialogues on the merits of certain shaving creams, the whole approach is self-serving and seductive.

Perfumes and ointments have always had a fascination for the human race. In biblical times, these luxuries were made to serve both good and evil purposes. They played a significant role in religious rituals but could also be condemned for gross misuse as when Isaiah, in a passage of stern rebuke, described wanton women of Jerusalem with their "perfume boxes" (Isa. 3:20, RSV). "Instead of a sweet smell," he said of these who pampered themselves and showed no concern for others, "there shall be stink" (v. 24).

The anonymous woman of Mark's story, whom we presume to have been Mary—sister to Lazarus (John 12:1-8)—displayed complete unselfishness when she devoted that expensive flask of oriental nard to her beloved guest. The aroma of the precious ointment filled the house (v. 3). But it was this woman's loving and perceptive action, in parting with perhaps her most valuable possession to honor Jesus, both in life and death, that filled "the whole world" with fragrance. Now that the incarnate Christ is with us no more, His other body—the church—should be the object of generous, sacrificial giving.

Traitor in the Midst

Mark 14:12-21

Jesus had a friend in Jerusalem, one who knew how to keep a confidence. In spite of the danger involved, he agreed to make "a large upper room furnished" (v. 15) available to our Lord where He could celebrate Passover with His disciples. None of the twelve, apparently, knew of this secret rendezvous. They were directed to it by a prearranged signal, a man (of all people!) carrying a water pitcher. The circle of hatred that surrounded the Master was being drawn so tight that fewer and fewer could be trusted to know where He was at any given time.

Within the hospitable walls of the upper room He would surely be safe from betrayal. Yet not so, for among those who sat around the memorial table was Judas, a disciple who had already sold out to the enemy. And beside Judas there was Peter, who was to carry a sword into Gethsemane to defend his Master and yet needed to be warned of a moment of approaching cowardice and denial. And beside Judas and Peter there were ten other men who, at the news of treachery in their ranks, self-consciously asked, "Is it I? . . . Is it I?" (v. 19).

Not many years later, the most loyal of our Lord's followers was to admit: "The good that I would I do not: but the evil which I would not, that I do" (Rom. 7:19). In the best of us there lurks a potential for repudiating not only the things we believe but the great object of our belief, the Lord Jesus Christ Himself. In recognition of our personal weakness, the prayer of hymn writer H. M. Butler may well be ours:

> Above the swamps of subterfuge and shame,
> The deeds, the thoughts, that honour may not name,
> The halting tongue that dares not tell the whole,
> O Lord of truth, lift every Christian soul.

Future Feasting
Matthew 26:26-35

Supposing our Lord to have followed the prescribed prayers for the Passover meal, He led His disciples in repeating these words, "Blessed art thou, Jehovah, King of the universe, who hast preserved us alive and sustained us and brought us to this season!" He may well have modified the formality of the traditional language (for was it not His practice to address God as "Father"?); but the thanksgiving for preservation to partake in yet another memorial meal matched His intention about to be disclosed.

A meal observed in remembrance of a past deliverance was about to be replaced by the shared bread and wine that would become the Christian memorial of another deliverance, greater by far. Jesus would become, in Paul's words, "our passover . . . sacrificed for us" (1 Cor. 5:7), God's new Lamb for the redemption of a new people. Only hours separated Him from the agony of the cross of which the bread and wine were eloquent symbols. Yet His final words, before leaving the security of the upper room for betrayal in Gethsemane, were not about the suffering that faced Him, but the triumph that would follow. "I will not drink henceforth of this fruit of the vine," he said, "until that day when I drink it new with you in my Father's kingdom" (v. 29).

With you! The Passover celebration could only look back to a day of salvation for a long-ago generation. The Lord's Supper, while inviting us to recall and be grateful for redemption accomplished, also bids us look forward to a great day of feasting to come. If we are qualified by faith to sit at the table where Christ's disciples share bread and wine, our names are on the guest list for that banquet in the heavenly kingdom.

(See *Day by Day with John,* pages 70-86.)

The Fifth Cup
Matthew 26:36-46

In a traditional observance of the Passover meal, a common cup was filled and emptied four times. So important was this part of the ritual that the poorest person was urged to provide for it, if necessary by pawning his coat or, failing that, with money from the poor box. The liquid content of the cup expressed the joy of those present over the memory of God's saving mercies. The passing of the cup from person to person emphasized the social participation by which each member of the assembled group was made to realize his oneness with the rest. Was it not with this in mind that our Master, when passing around "the cup of blessing" (1 Cor. 10:16), said to His friends, "Drink ye all of it," (Matt. 26:27)?

But there was a fifth cup. Of this, Jesus alone would drink. Concerning this, He prayed, "O my Father, if it be possible, let this cup pass from me" (v. 39). And again, "O my Father, if this cup may not pass away from me, except I drink it, thy will be done" (v. 42). That the disciples had no part in this cup was made plain by their failure to keep vigil with their Master. While He agonized in prayer, they slept. Soon, during His suffering on the cross, they would put a safe distance between themselves and danger. From the arrest in the garden to the hour of His death, Jesus was alone so far as human companionship was concerned. None could share the cup that He must drink.

Blame might be attached to men who failed their Lord in His time of crisis. But greater blame belongs to those who suppose that they are in command of their spiritual destinies. The fifth cup should remind us all that there are some things we cannot do for ourselves, the greatest of which is to win salvation. This is why it is written, "While we were still weak, . . . Christ died for the ungodly" (Rom. 5:6, RSV).

Runaway Swordsman

Matthew 26:47-56

That eminent Scottish preacher, Arthur J. Gossip, made use of his picturesque national vocabulary when he described the Gethsemane swordsman's action as "a daft thing to do." An unsheathed sword was an invitation to violent reaction by our Lord's enemies, imperiling the lives of the disciples and the sacred cause with which they were to be entrusted. When, thanks to John's Gospel, we learn that Peter wielded that rash weapon (18:10), we recognize a characteristic impetuosity that again and again provided contrast between good intention and poor judgment.

What Christian can fail to be disturbed by the knowledge that the man who struck a blow (however poorly aimed) for his Master was almost immediately afterward included in that ignoble company of whom it is recorded: "All the disciples forsook him, and fled" (v. 56)? Courage soon gave place to cowardice, leaving our Lord to face His accusers in utter loneliness, deserted by His closest friends.

A string of philosophers and poets have played with a debatable idea that was expressed in Goldsmith's lines, "For he who fights and runs away/ May live to fight another day." Another poet, A. E. Housman, showed keener perception when he wrote of "the man that runs away" that he lives "to die another day." We may be sure that the remorse that overtook Peter was not relieved by the memory of one uncautious moment when he lopped off the ear of the high priest's servant. For it is not in isolated deeds of loyalty that true discipleship proves itself but in that continuing faithfulness that persists when pressures mount and dangers threaten. Peter was to find his inspiration to this kind of loyalty in Jesus Himself who "suffered for us, leaving us an example, that ye should follow his steps" (1 Pet. 2:21).

Whose the Guilt?

Matthew 26:57-68

History's pages are blemished with the names of persons who earned fame by their infamy. Caligula, Torquemada, and the marquis de Sade are notorious examples. The atrocities attributed to Torquemada are the more reprehensible since he held religious orders. Office in the church did not restrain him from committing widespread injustice and cruelty as head of the Inquisition in Spain. His fifteenth-century campaign against heretics was, in fact, carried out in the name of religion.

Caiaphas, too, was a reputedly religious man. His appointment as high priest was made by the Roman authorities, but he could only function by subscribing to and practicing the requirements of the Jewish faith. These, however, placed no curb on his persecuting zeal; for once he had resolved to rid his realm of Jesus of Nazareth, he allowed no barriers of law or custom to stand in his way. Our Lord's ecclesiastical trial, which took place in Caiaphas's official residence, was stained by numerous irregularities, including disregard of the universal principle that an accused person should be assumed innocent until proved otherwise.

Unfortunately, when religious intolerance is in the seat of power, a plea of innocence is likely to gain no hearing. Our Lord clearly recognized this, for He remained silent before the testimony of false witnesses. But His silence was broken when called upon to speak for Himself. He affirmed His messiahship and countered the prejudiced proceedings of Caiaphas and his court with a prediction concerning His coming to ultimate power. That prospect should have caused His enemies to tremble, for it declared their accountability before God for the dastardly deed in which they were engaged. For us, it is our Lord's own assurance of a future in which "he will not fail or be discouraged/till he has established justice in the earth" (Isa. 42:4, RSV).

"Warts and All"
Luke 22:54-62

Not all of God's heroes have been persons of steellike constancy. Abraham twice showed a lack of moral responsibility when he felt threatened by his wife's beauty. Jacob continued to live up to his reputation as "a grabber" until late in life he decided to let God take control. David, for all his evaluation as a "man after God's own heart," surrendered to expediency and lust to achieve selfish ends. And amazingly enough, it is the Bible itself which acquaints us with the blemishes of character in these and other of its outstanding personalities.

One might expect that the early church would suppress the lapses of the apostle Peter and not mention them repeatedly in the Gospel records. But what despondency would overwhelm us if the men and women of Scripture were all paragons of virtue! As it is, the honesty of the Word of God in portraying its personalities, "warts and all," to magnify the grace of God in its abounding patience and pardon gives us hope for acceptance in spite of our unworthiness.

When in the Marian persecutions that followed the death of Henry VIII, Thomas Cranmer was condemned to a fiery death, he was given permission to address the assembled crowds on the supposition that he would justify his executioners. Instead, he expressed remorse for weakness under threat of penalty by putting his signature to documents that violated his conscience. As he thrust his right hand into the flames he confessed to its many offences, "writing contrary to my heart," in consequence of which, he said, "it shall be first burned." Cranmer's belated repentance could not undo the wrongs he had committed but did affirm the man's basic integrity. To Peter, and to us, the opportunity is given to make amends for errors of the past and give living testimony to God's pardoning and restoring grace.

Silence in Court!

Matthew 27:1-2,11-26

Does it seem strange that the Master remained silent while His enemies accused Him and Pilate plied Him with questions? Could it be that He was waiting for someone to step forward and speak in His defence?

There is an ancient story that, during the trial before Pilate, a learned man came forward and asked leave to speak. He identified himself as Nicodemus, member of the Sanhedrin, and in earnest words pleaded for Jesus' life. Then, encouraged by his action, one after another stepped forward from the crowd. "I was lame, and Jesus healed me." "I touched the hem of his garment and was made whole." "I was born blind but Jesus pitied me and gave me sight." And another said, "My son was dying when I besought Jesus to help me, and my son was healed in that selfsame hour." Thus one by one they stood tall and testified for Jesus so that Pilate was impressed and sought ways to release His prisoner.

Alas, this is only a story. When our Lord most needed a friendly voice to speak for Him, not one was raised. Of the many who had been blessed at His hands, none were ready to respond in gratitude. Well might He have expressed His disappointment in words of an old-time prophet, "I have trodden the winepress alone; and of the people there was none with me" (Isa. 63:3).

Theologically, His loneliness, in those hours when redemption's work was coming to completion, speaks impressively of the unaided activity of God in dealing with the problem of sin. But at the level of our responsibility we should feel the shame of knowing that, in this time of supreme crisis, neither love nor loyalty raised hand or voice in His support. In a true sense, Jesus Christ is still on trial at the bar of human opinion. Shall I remain silent, or shall I speak?

Blessed Conscript
Matthew 27:27-37

Pilate's vacillation in condemning Jesus was not reflected in the behavior of the soldiers who carried out his orders. Once the sentence of crucifixion had been pronounced, the gentle Christ became the property of men whose trade had brutalized them. Before they led Him forth to death, they humiliated Him by making Him the subject of their cruel sport when they ridiculed His claim to kingship. At the place called Golgotha, they routinely played their parts in the most degrading method of execution the human mind has ever devised. After which, so it is written, "sitting down they watched him there" (v. 36).

One thing stands to their credit, and that only because as so often happens, God allowed the wrath of men to praise Him. Exercising their authority as the emperor's men, they conscripted a bystander to carry the cross for Jesus. Unintentionally, by an act of military coercion, they also enlisted a family into the service of the church. Perhaps Simon of Cyrene himself, but certainly his sons Alexander and Rufus, became prominent among Christ's followers, well-known enough for their names to find a place in the gospel record (Mark 15:21).

Simon had no choice in the ministry he performed. Doubtless he was rewarded by a grateful look or gracious word from the physically-exhausted Savior, and these alone could have stirred a saving faith. But the burden he bore for Jesus was not willingly assumed. It was thrust upon him with no opportunity for refusal. The cross of discipleship, on the other hand, must be shouldered voluntarily. "If any man will come after me," said Jesus, "let him . . . take up his cross, and follow me" (Matt. 16:24). Only the compulsion of love can produce such response, and where is that compulsion stronger than at the place where Jesus died?

Promise of Paradise
Luke 23:35-43

How much our Lord's partners in death knew about Him, we cannot tell. Such knowledge as they had may have come from the derisive shouts to which the dying Savior was subjected. Some of the calloused observers called Him Christ only to question his right to that exalted title. Others, quoting the inscription Pilate had ordered placed above His head, challenged Him to prove Himself "king of the Jews" by coming down from the cross (v. 38). Could it be that what were taunts on the lips of the Master's enemies were transformed into vehicles of hope for one of the thieves? Perhaps by the operation of divine grace that is beyond our understanding, titles of great dignity that were flung in mockery in the face of the Son of God became the substance of faith for a poor wretch expiring beside Him. "Lord," he cried, with a sincerity that none around him shared, "remember me when thou comest into thy kingdom" (v. 42).

The response was at once extraordinary and commonplace. It was commonplace in that it employed a word taken from the popular religious vocabulary of the times. Adopted from the Persians, "paradise" described a garden of great beauty and was accordingly appropriate for a bygone Garden of Eden or the prospective felicities of heaven. Using a term, therefore, that the dying thief understood (theological niceties would only have confused him), Jesus made His response extraordinary by promising not a place in a faraway kingdom but his companionship in an immediate paradise. "To-day shalt thou be with me in paradise" (v. 43). As "in the cool of the day," God had walked the paths of Eden seeking the company of the man and woman He had made, so, beyond the mutual distress of dying, the exalted Jesus and a re-created brigand would enjoy sweet fellowship in a place we know as heaven.

Darkness and Light
Mark 15:33-41

Nature pulled the shades throughout those dreadful hours when the Lord of nature hung dying on the cross. There was "darkness over the whole land" (v. 33). Who can wonder that the sun withdrew its light while human commitment to sin expressed itself in its most vicious form? Who would be surprised that it should hide its eyes from the spectacle of the Son of God exposed to indignity and pain on a gibbet designed for the worst of criminals?

Darkness also reigned in the minds of those who perpetrated this awful deed. When the dying Jesus cried out to His Father, they supposed that He was calling for Elijah. That prophet had a reputation for coming to the aid of persons in distress. But these hardhearted onlookers doubted that Elijah would respond, though they said (perhaps in sport) that they were willing to wait and see. That God should have any interest in what was going on had no place in their thinking.

For one brief moment, Jesus Himself seemed plunged into darkness. He had dreaded this moment as in the Garden of Gethsemane He prayed, "Abba, Father, . . . take away this cup from me" (14:36). As our sinbearer, He knew that the judgment we should bear would become His. Immersed in a sea of iniquity that was not His but ours, did He sense the indescribable loneliness of being cut off from the presence of a holy God? We cannot tell for certain. We only hear that agonized cry, "My God, my God, why hast thou forsaken me?" (v. 34) and interpret it as best we can.

In all this darkness, a light from heaven shone to illumine the mind of the centurion in charge. "Truly this man was the Son of God," he exclaimed (v. 39), a response that the Gospel writers seek from all their readers.

A Secret No More

Matthew 27:57-66

Few New Testament characters have gathered a body of legend greater than Joseph of Arimathaea. We are asked to believe, for example, that after the burial of Jesus, this man took the cup used at the Last Supper, carried it to England, and founded at Glastonbury the first Christian church in that land. This is a pretty story but without foundation in fact. What is known about Joseph is written into the Gospel narratives, each of the four evangelists contributing to the portrait of one who although rich and influential identified in a significant way with the rejected, condemned, and crucified Man of Galilee. He did this, Matthew tells us, because he "was Jesus' disciple" (v. 57). To this information the apostle John added his own comment: "but secretly for fear of the Jews" (John 19:38).

We may feel regret that John thought it necessary to make that addition. Yet what an exposure it provides of our own frequent suppression of public witness to Jesus Christ! For fear of many things, some weighty and others trifling, testimony to belief in the Master is withheld—and always to our shame. Joseph must have spent many miserable days forbidding his lips to voice what his heart wanted to say. There was at least one occasion when he was moved to action, but it was negative action. He did not vote with his fellow members of the Sanhedrin when they condemned Jesus to death (Luke 23:51).

What, then, gave Joseph courage at last to go public? Surely it was the cross itself with its demonstration of "love so amazing, so divine" that compelled a secret disciple into open confession. When the flame of our own devotion flickers and threatens to die, a journey to Calvary should fan it into brightness and warmth. Let us say again, with Paul: "the Son of God, who loved me, and gave himself for me" (Gal. 2:20).

Muted Trumpets
Mark 16:1-11

Most churches have at least one person in their member-ship who can be depended on to raise divisive questions in business sessions. A pastor of Riverside Church, New York City, told of one such person. This lady was invariably present and possessed a rare talent for creating friction. At one particular meeting, to the pastor's delight, she seemed to have herself under control. But toward the end, she in-dicated her desire to speak. She stood and demanded, "What happened to the trumpets on Easter Sunday?"

Nobody could deny that, this time, the belligerent mem-ber had asked a good question. For years at Riverside Church, the practice had been to open the Easter morning service with a chorus of trumpets. For some reason that year, the trumpets had been left out. To the objector, Easter Sun-day morning was not Easter Sunday morning without trum-pets.

If we accept that Mark's authentic record ends with verse 8—the remaining verses being a later addition—there were no trumpets on the first resurrection morning. Instead, it is written of the disciples that "they were afraid" (v. 8). The news was simply too good to be true. But doubts and fears gave place to glad confidence that, as Peter said, "This Jesus hath God raised up, whereof we all are witnesses" (Acts 2:32). From that time to this, the message of the Christian church concerns a crucified and risen Savior. In the absence of trumpets, can we not (should we not) take up the ancient Christian greeting for Easter Day and tell the whole, wide world that Christ is risen?

Let's Go Home!
Luke 24:13-32

A normal reaction to a disappointing experience, whether a wet day, a poor concert performance, or an unproductive shopping spree, is: "Let's go home!" Cleopas and his companion (could they have been husband and wife?) felt that way. They had gone to Jerusalem for the Passover and also with the hope of seeing Jesus, of whom they were humble followers. The feast, they had assumed, might well provide the occasion for a display of messianic authority of Jesus' part. Instead, He had submitted without resistance to His enemies, and before the Passover sabbath dawned, had breathed His last on a Roman cross. True, rumors were current in the city that he had been raised from the dead. But to these two, as even to the intimate circle of the disciples, these seemed "as idle tales" (v. 11).

"Let's go home" they said, as though in familiar surroundings they might forget their sorrow, or view it in a better light. But putting miles between them and Jerusalem did nothing to relieve their distress. They fussed at one another as they walked and, when a Stranger joined them, were less than courteous when He inquired about their obvious gloom. Then, in a fashion surpassing that of any rabbi they had known He opened up the Scriptures to help them understand the glorious mystery of the suffering Savior.

Entranced but not persuaded, they reached their home and bade the Stranger be their guest. There in the simple act of giving thanks for a shared meal, He revealed His identity. Not in the Temple or synagogue, not in the upper room or on some quiet retreat, but in the familiar setting of home Jesus wiped away their tears and filled their hearts with unspeakable joy and their lips with a message of joy for others.

Table Fellowship
Luke 24:33-43

In his summation of the postresurrection appearances of our Lord, Luke declared that "he shewed himself alive . . . by many infallible proofs" (Acts 1:3). The setting for at least three of these appearances was a meal. At Emmaus, Jesus opened the tear-dimmed eyes of His hosts as He prayed over food. Later that same day in Jerusalem, He apparently intruded upon His disciples as they dined and, in their presence, ate "a piece of broiled fish" to show that He was no ghost but had a body of "flesh and bones" (vv. 39,42). And according to John 21, He had table fellowship with seven of His disciples after He had enabled those frustrated fishermen to fill their net with fish.

These incidents, of course, raise the question of the nature of our Lord's resurrection body. Many have sought to probe the mystery without success. Yet those who witnessed His comings and goings—sometimes regardless of physical laws, at others in obedience to them—accepted these phenomena not as reasons for doubting the reality of His resurrection, but as evidences for it. He showed them the wounds in His hands and feet, then ate in their presence that they might know that He who died for them was now alive forevermore. And by the very act of eating with them, he Exemplified that unbroken fellowship between disciple and Lord begun in the days of His flesh and to be continued until the feasting begins in the eternal realm.

But we need not look back with envy of those who were blessed with His companionship in the past, nor await impatiently the coming festivities of heaven. For John in Patmos has passed on the gracious invitation of the ascended Lord, "If any man hear my voice, and open the door, I will come in to him, and will sup with him, and he with me" (Rev. 3:20).

(See *Day by Day with John* pages 96-99.)

Amazing Grace!
Matthew 28:16-20; Luke 24:44-53

During those amazing forty days in which the risen Christ revealed Himself to His disciples, He maintained contact with them whether they were in Jerusalem or Galilee. But the final rendezvous was Jerusalem where He charged His followers to remain "until ye be endued with power from on high" (Luke 24:49). Though it was in Galilee that he gave the Great Commission, it was in the Holy City that He amplified it. The gospel message was still to be proclaimed "among all nations," but with the important proviso that this saving witness should have its "beginning at Jerusalem" (Luke 24:47).

In 1558, when the French port of Calais was lost to the English, the reigning queen, Mary, said that after her death the word *Calais* would be found written on her heart. Her attachment to that city did not have the noblest motivation. How different it was with Jesus whose affection for Jerusalem was expressed in tears (Luke 19:41) and survived the cruel death that He suffered at the hands of its leaders. In parting words to his disciples he spoke that city's name and bade them place its interests first in their program of world evangelism.

Bunyan marveled at this when, in *The Jerusalem Sinner Saved,* he wrote: "One would have thought, since the Jerusalem sinners were the worst and greatest sinners, . . . that He should rather have said, Go into all the world, and preach repentance and remission of sins among all nations; and, *after* that, offer the same to Jerusalem; yea, it had been infinite grace if He had said so. But what grace is this, or what name shall we give it, when He commands that this repentance and remission of sins, which is designed to be preached in all nations, should first be offered to Jerusalem; in the first place to the worst of sinners!"

Maran-atha!
Acts 1:1-14

There was mystery in His coming and His going—not the mystery of the occult that engenders fear but divine mystery that induces awe and reverence and adoration. He came in accordance with physical law, "made of a woman," as Paul wrote (Gal. 4:4), yet without the help of a man. He left this world not through the dread gateway of death—for He arose from the grave—but by a royal route that bore Him heavenward in the sight of wondering disciples.

Yet, for all this, He retained the common touch to the very end. On reliable authority we may believe that at the mount of His ascension, where He is described as "being assembled together with" His disciples, the true meaning is that once again, and for the last time, "he was eating a meal with them" (v. 4, Phillips). He went, as it were, from a picnic with friends to the banquet hall of His Father in heaven.

But this world has not seen the last of Him. Peter, on the day of Pentecost, foresaw a coming day of triumph for the crucified Son of God. Quoting a psalm, he said, "The Lord said unto my Lord, Sit thou on my right hand, Until I make thy foes thy footstool" (Acts 2:34-35). Even more explicitly, in another Temple sermon he spoke of coming "times of refreshing" that would arrive when God "shall send Jesus Christ, . . . Whom the heaven must receive until the times of restitution of all things" (3:19-21).

The early church made two Aramaic words—*Maran-atha* —a confession of faith that looked both backward and forward. *Maran-atha* can mean "the Lord has come" or "the Lord will come," so it became a witness to the Christ of the incarnation and the second advent. "Even so, come, Lord Jesus" (Rev. 22:20) is our prayer and *Maran-atha* our testimony.